Tuning the Kingdom

Eastman/Rochester Studies
in Ethnomusicology

Ellen Koskoff, Senior Editor
Eastman School of Music
(ISSN: 2161-0290)

Burma's Pop Music Industry:
Creators, Distributors, Censors
Heather MacLachlan

Yorùbá Music in the Twentieth Century:
Identity, Agency and Performance Practice
Bode Omojola

Javanese Gamelan and the West
Sumarsam

Gender in Chinese Music
Edited by Rachel Harris, Rowan Pease, and Shzr Ee Tan

Performing Gender, Place, and Emotion in Music:
Global Perspectives
Edited by Fiona Magowan and Louise Wrazen

Music, Indigeneity, Digital Media
Edited by Thomas R. Hilder, Henry Stobart, and Shzr Ee Tan

Listen with the Ear of the Heart:
Music and Monastery Life at Weston Priory
Maria S. Guarino

Tuning the Kingdom:
Kawuugulu Musical Performance, Politics, and Storytelling in Buganda
Damascus Kafumbe

Tuning the Kingdom

Kawuugulu Musical Performance, Politics, and Storytelling in Buganda

Damascus Kafumbe

UNIVERSITY OF ROCHESTER PRESS

The University of Rochester Press gratefully acknowledges generous support from the AMS 75 PAYS Endowment of the American Musicological Society, funded in part by the National Endowment for the Humanities and the Andrew W. Mellon Foundation; the Pabst Charitable Foundation for the Arts; Middlebury College; and the Research and Publication Award of the Society for Ethnomusicology.

First published 2018

University of Rochester Press
668 Mt. Hope Avenue, Rochester, NY 14620, USA
www.urpress.com
and Boydell & Brewer Limited
PO Box 9, Woodbridge, Suffolk IP12 3DF, UK
www.boydellandbrewer.com

ISBN-13: 978-1-58046-904-3
ISSN: 2161-0290

Library of Congress Cataloging-in-Publication Data

Names: Kafumbe, Damascus, author.
Title: Tuning the kingdom : Kawuugulu musical performance, politics, and
    storytelling in Buganda / Damascus Kafumbe.
Other titles: Eastman/Rochester studies in ethnomusicology ; v. 8.
Description: Rochester : University of Rochester Press, 2018. | Series: Eastman/
    Rochester studies in ethnomusicology, ISSN 2161-0290 ; v. 8 | Includes
    bibliographical references and index.
Identifiers: LCCN 2017055861 | ISBN 9781580469043 (hardcover : alk. paper)
Subjects: LCSH: Music—Social aspects—Uganda—Buganda. | Music and identity
    politics—Uganda—Buganda.
Classification: LCC ML3917.U33 K34 2018 | DDC 781.62/963957—dc23 LC record
    available at https://lccn.loc.gov/2017055861

This publication is printed on acid-free paper.
Printed in the United States of America.

To the memory of my maternal granduncle Kabenge Gombe (1931–2016), for facilitating my access to Kawuugulu

Contents

Illustrations

Figures

Musical Examples

Acknowledgments

So many people have directly and indirectly contributed to the fruition of this book that it is impossible to mention all of their individual contributions. Here I acknowledge the most important, in alphabetical order, and express my gratitude to those I do not have space to list.

This book would not have been possible without the knowledge, experiences, hospitality, and support of the many Baganda with whom I have worked in different villages and towns of Uganda since the early 2000s.[1] I thank Agustino Serunkuma, Albert Bisaso, Albert Muwanga Ssempeke, Annet Najjuka, Mike Kasirye, Anthony Mugagga Muwagga, Asumani Luyuzambugo, Brenda Najjuka Nabagereka, Bulasio Katimbo, Christopher Mukasa Muteeweta, Costa Nakyagaba, Daniel Mukasa Wagaba Sebiyenje, Daudi Kigozi, Deogratio Semugooma, Diriisa Kasiga, Edward Ng'anda Mujuuli, Erasmus Kyagaba Binywera, Esther Grace Nabagereka, Filomena Namusoke, Florence Nakyazze, Francis Bbirikkadde, Francis Walakira, Fredrick Bombo, Fredrick Kaggwa Semugooma, George Lutwama, George William Kalyemenya, George William Mayombwe, Ggunju Matia Kawere, Goreti Nalugunju, Gustavus Adulphus Lukonge, Hamidu Sekweyama, Hannington Joshua Kizza Mugwanya, Herbert Mulasa Bbirikkadde Musiitwa, Idi Semulya Kasirye Lunaanoba, Ignatio Kawere Ganaayaba, Jamaada Maviirinkata, John Musoke Mubanda Sekibaala, Joseph Sekandi, Joseph Walugembe, Joseph Zimula, Kabenge Gombe, Kafeero Mukasa, Kasalina Nalubowa, Kasonko Nkaawu Mugunda, Laurencio Kityo, Leonard Kisaaliita, Livingstone Kaggwa Lule Mafumu, Ludovico Semuwemba Serwanga, Yesoni Nsereko, Maria Luiza Ntudde, Mary Namukwaya, Mary Nancy Najjuka, Mikayiri Kawere, Moses Musisi Magonge, Moses Sserwadda, Mubarak Zimula, Nnaalongo Zaituni Namukasa Nakku, Norah Elvania Namugga, Nuulu Nakafeero Walusimbi, Omukongozzi Luwedde Mpogola, Omukongozzi Mulondo, Omukongozzi Nakibinge, Paulo Kabwama, Paulo Mwanje Muwanga, Peter Kinene, Pius Sempa Kawere, Rashid Zimula, Simeo Ssemmambo Sebuwuufu, Ssaalongo Charles Lutaaya Muwaga, Ssaalongo Chrisostom Sebuliba, Ssaalongo Deziderio Kiwanuka Matovu, Ssaalongo Matia Senfuma, Ssaalongo Muhammad Katimbo Sensonga, Ssaalongo Samwiri Bakkabulindi, Ssaalongo Ssenoga Majwaala, Steven Mukasa Kabugo, Steven Wagaba, Tereeza Nabunnya, Umaru Mukasa Kavuma, Venancio Mukasa Wagaba, Waalabyekyi

Magoba, Wilfred Mugwanya Kabuusu, Wilson Sekabira, Yekoyaada Kaggwa Kyagaba, Yisaaya Ng'anda, and Yozefiina Nakitto.

Special thanks also to the following organizations for funding the research for this book: the American Musicological Society, Florida State University College of Music, Middlebury College, Pabst Charitable Foundation for the Arts, and Society for Ethnomusicology.

I am equally grateful to the Akugoba Drum Makers, Butiko Clan, Central Broadcasting Services, Ggaba National Seminary, Kabaka Foundation, Kyambogo University, Makerere University, Mbogo Drum Producers, Mmengo Palace, Sikyomu Drum Makers, Uganda Museum, Uganda National Cultural Center, and Uganda Society for agreeing to participate in the research.

Thanks also to Betty Castor, Hiram Powell, Joann Andersen, Margery Pabst, Samuel Bell III, and members of the Redeemed Christian Church of God International Chapel and Mosaic Church in Tallahassee for supporting me and my family while I was in the field.

I wish to express my gratitude also to the custodians of the royal tombs of the kings of the past associated with Kawuugulu, particularly the royal tombs of Ssekabaka Mulondo, Ssekabaka Kateregga, Ssekabaka Muteesa I, Ssekabaka Mwanga II, Ssekabaka Cwa II, and Ssekabaka Muteesa II, for their cooperation.

Many thanks to the editorial staff at the University of Rochester Press, including Sonia Kane, editorial director; Ellen Koskoff, Eastman/Rochester Studies in Ethnomusicology series editor; and Julia Cook, associate editor, as well as outside readers for believing in this book and helping it get published.

The book would have turned out differently without the input of many colleagues who provided editorial comments on its earlier versions or chapters. I am very thankful to Ann Lucas, Bret Woods, Carol Muller, David Locke, Douglass Seaton, Elizabeth Clendinning, Frank Gunderson, Gerhard Kubik, Greg Vitercik, Holly Hansen, Jacob Tropp, Jean Kidula, Jennifer Kyker, Joseph Hellweg (who suggested the idea of performative constitution), Katie Stufflebeam, Larry Hamberlin, Lois Anderson, Lucas Avidan, Matthew Morin, Michael Uzendoski, Peter Cooke, Peter Hamlin, Peter Hoesing, Rebecca Dirksen, Rebecca Mitchell, Su Tan, and Sylvia A. Nannyonga-Tamusuza.

Many thanks to my student research assistants for their various contributions to this project. I am grateful to Anna LaSala-Goettler, Dante Francomano, Hannah Dietrich, Jack Herscowitz, Lucas Avidan, Mary Grace Gately, and William Hardcastle for helping with secondary research and/or copyediting; Samuel Kudman for recreating all musical examples in Sibelius; and Kenton Ratliff for creating professional figures: P.1, P.2, P.3, I.1, I.2, I.3, and 5.1.

Deep thanks also to my family members. I owe the biggest debt to my best friend and dear wife, Betty, for taking care of our lovely sons Joshua, Jonathan, and Joseph while I worked away on the project. Her sacrifices and many contributions to the project have allowed me complete it, including her assistance in transcribing interviews and music, translating Luganda text, proofreading, and copyediting. And I owe a big debt to the boys for being patient and understanding. I will forever be grateful to my late maternal granduncle Kabenge Gombe for facilitating my access to Kawuugulu and helping hone my understanding of the ensemble's sociopolitical importance. I am very thankful also for the mentorship and support of my dear parents, Fred and Ruth Serunkuma, as well as siblings, Herbert Kinobe, Richard Sewagudde, James Kiwuwa, Esther Ntabadde, and Miriam Nakiyinji. I am grateful to my sisters-in-law Francisca Nakachwa and Cathy Nakanwagi, both of whom have served as my research assistants. And I am equally grateful to my parents-in-law, Simon and Theodora Yiga, and family friends John and Susan Bukenya, for being wonderful hosts in Uganda.

Finally, I am unendingly thankful to the Almighty God for the gifts of life and grace.

Note on Translation, Transliteration, and Orthography

Luganda, a Bantu language, is the official tongue of the Baganda people of Buganda. It is also the primary language in which I conducted all the fieldwork that informs this project. Luganda text and words appear in italics with the exception of proper nouns, including names of ensembles, groups, places, and institutions or organizations. Titles of songs and dances as well as names of the performance sections or movements in which they are featured are styled according to standard usages: They are in roman type, within quotation marks, followed by a translation of the title or name in parentheses. All titles preceding proper names are capitalized. For example, *ssekabaka* = deceased king, Ssekabaka Mulondo = Deceased King Mulondo; *kabaka* = king, Kabaka Mutebi II = King Mutebi II. Names of drums and non-musical instruments that are treated as proper names also have initial uppercase letters; they are italicized to distinguish them from other types of proper names.

The Luganda consonants used in this book are *b, c, d, f, g, h, j, k, l, m, n, p, r, s, t, v, w, y, z*, and *ŋ*, which has a velar nasal sound similar to the sound at the end of the English word "ding." Contemporary keyboards do not have the consonant *ŋ*, so some Luganda speakers replace it with the digraph *ng* followed by an apostrophe (*ng'*).

The pronunciation of a consonant depends on the vowel that follows it, and this determines meaning. The tonal range and length of the vowels *a* ("ah"), *e* ("eh"), *i* ("ee'), *o* ("oh"), and *u* ("oo") shape the tonal character and the meaning of all Luganda terms used in the book. Double vowels create long sounds, such as in the ensemble name Kawuugulu. Initial vowels *a, e,* and *o* serve as agglutinative letters that indicate articles and prefix forms of infinitives in the case of verbs, as in the following examples:

e + *ŋŋoma* (drum) = *eŋŋoma* ("a drum"; "the drum"; "drum"; "drums").
A + Baganda ("natives of Buganda") = Abaganda ("the Baganda").

o + *kubina* ("dancing while jumping and lifting legs very high") = *okubina* ("to dance while jumping and lifting legs very high").

I use English articles "the" and "a" with some noun stems, and in such instances I omit the initial vowel. Thus, "*empuunyi* drum" becomes "the *mpuunyi* drum."

Consonant sounds vary depending on how they are combined. Double consonants indicate stressed and longer approximant consonant sounds, such as the *jj* digraph in the drum name *Kasajja*. The *ny* combination, such as in the drum name *Nyamitongo*, may act as a syllable and as a nasal consonant. The *ky* digraph sounds like the consonant *c* (pronounced "ch"), although *c* has a shorter sound than *ky*. Consequently, double vowels usually follow *c*; an example is the name of the first section or movement of a Kawuugulu performance, "Kaaciica," while a single vowel follows *ky*, such as in the name of the Butiko (Mushroom) Clan forefather, Kyebagaba. When *ky* appears in a closing syllable of a word, such as in the town name Kamwokya, it normally has a short sound. Although the combination *ggy* in the closing syllable of *luggya* (quaternary clan lineage) and *jj* in the drum name *Kasajja* may sound similar, some contemporary Luganda speakers pronounce them slightly differently. *Ggya* can sound like "gea" in the English word "gear," while *jja* sounds like "ja" in the English word "jar." The vowel *i* rarely follows the consonant *y* (which is also regarded as a semi-vowel) when the latter is preceded by a consonant. Thus, *okaggira* ("you uproot") versus *okaggyira* in the song "Akatiko aka Nnamulondo" (The *Nnamulondo* Mushroom). The consonant *r* sounds similar to the consonant *l.*

Last, the prefixes *mu, ba, ka, bu,* and *ki* are added to the stem *ganda* to signify various cultural aspects of the Baganda people:

Buganda = kingdom of the Baganda
Baganda = natives of Buganda
Luganda = language of the Baganda
Kiganda = adjectival descriptor for cultural norms and practices of the Baganda

Note on the Musical Examples

Throughout this book I use Western staff notation to illustrate pitches and rhythms of Kawuugulu music. However, conventional Western staff pitches do not capture traditional Kiganda pitch repertory accurately.[1] In addition, the Baganda use one verb, *kuyimba*, for both "to sing," and "to chant," and the noun *luyimba*, for "sung text" and "chanted text, which tends to resemble spoken text. I refer to chants as songs, but use a slash (/) to represent chanted text, which Kawuugulu performs as stylized speech with louder, clearer enunciation and often higher tessitura. I use regular headnotes or standard pitch symbols to represent sung text and "open tones" of drums.[2] Ensemble members tune these drums carefully to specific pitches. For instance, the open tones of the *Nyamitongo* drum pair tend to sound an octave above those of the *Kawuugulu* and *Kasajja* drum pair, whereas the *mpuunyi* drum's open tone tends to sound approximately a fourth interval below the *Kasajja* drum (both shown in example 5.1). I use *x*'s to represent sounds of pellet bells, which produce indeterminate and almost monotone pitches.

The Luganda titles of some musical examples imply more than they say. My translations convey the meaning as understood by the local people, both literal and nonliteral meanings. For instance, "dances" is implied in example 2.3, as are "ankle bells," "performers," "abode," and "amniotic" in examples 2.4, 2.5, 2.6, and 4.1.

Preface

A Kingdom in and out of Tune

Kawuugulu is arguably the oldest and longest surviving drum, song, and dance ensemble of the Ugandan Kingdom of Buganda. From precolonial times through missionization and colonialism and into the postcolonial era, the ensemble has managed, structured, modeled, and legitimized power relations in the kingdom. Enduring Muslim and Christian evangelization, British colonial rule, and post-independence violence and tyranny, Kawuugulu has served as an archive, "entextualization," and aide-mémoire of Buganda's clan and royal history.[1] Despite the ensemble's long existence and continuing political importance, however, it has received little academic or nonacademic documentation. For centuries, most narratives about Kawuugulu have remained the secrets of Aboobutiko, primary members of the Butiko, or Mushroom, Clan, and of individuals with whom the clan has close kinship. Through maternal ties to the clan established at birth, I have been able to gain unique access to Kawuugulu and its stories, making it possible for me to conduct the first in-depth study of this centuries-old ensemble and its connections to sociopolitical life in Buganda.[2]

I draw on oral and written accounts, archival research, and musical analysis to argue that Kawuugulu uses musical performance and storytelling that integrates human and nonhuman stories to sustain a complex sociopolitical hierarchy that interweaves and balances kin and clan ties in delicate tension with royal prerogatives. In referring to this phenomenon as "tuning the kingdom" I allude to its similarity to the process of tensioning or stretching (*kuleega*) drum hides. The process is ongoing, as the drums are always moving between, in, and out of tune. Also, as the Baganda say, *Eŋŋoma gye bazireegera si gye zivugira*: The drums do not sound as when they were tuned.[3] As Kawuugulu adapts to the rapidly changing world around it, this book is important for cataloging how it has historically shaped principles of the three inextricably related domains that build the backbone of Kiganda politics: kinship, clanship, and kingship.

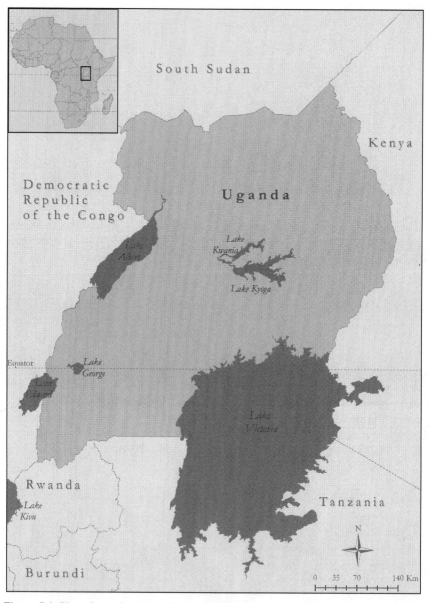

Figure P.1. Uganda and surrounding countries.

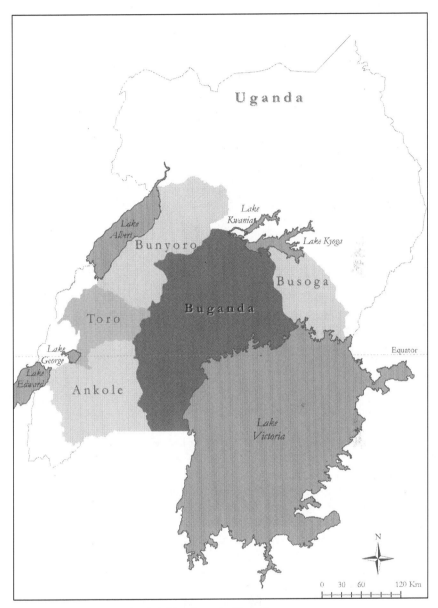

Figure P.2. Buganda and other kingdoms in Uganda.

Buganda, the geographical focus of this book, is located in south-central Uganda, a sub-Saharan East African country that spans the Equator, south of South Sudan, east of the Democratic Republic of the Congo, north of Rwanda and Tanzania, and west of Kenya (see fig. P.1). The Kingdom of Buganda is one of Uganda's five interlacustrine Bantu kingdoms (see fig. P.2).[4]

The origins of Buganda are unclear, but the historians E. S. Atieno Odhiambo, T. I. Ouso, and J. F. M. Williams suggest that the kingdom originated from Bantu clans dating back as far as AD 1000.[5] According to one origin story, the first hereditary leader of Buganda was originally an entrepreneur from the Kingdom of Bunyoro, where his name was Kato ("Younger male twin") Ruhuuga.[6] After retaking the administration of Buganda around the early fourteenth century, Kato requested knowledgeable people of Buganda, the Baganda, to reveal to him the most revered person in Buganda. They identified the legendary Kintu, whom many still hold in high esteem as their forefather and the originator of the non-nomadic people commonly known as Baanabaakintu ("Children of Kintu") and whom some confuse with Kato Ruhuuga. The valued status of the legendary Kintu and his wife Nambi impressed Kato Ruhuuga so much that he asked the people of Buganda to rename him Kintu. Similarly, he requested them to rename his wife Nantuttululu Nambi. They granted these requests, given Kato Ruhuuga's outstanding leadership and reputation in uniting Baganda. From that time forth, he permanently became known as Kintu.[7]

Because most of the history about Buganda's origins has been transmitted orally, there are discrepancies and lack of clarity in understanding Kintu's role in forming the Kingdom of Buganda and the sociopolitical circumstances of its formation, as the ethnomusicologist Sylvia A. Nannyonga-Tamusuza points out.[8] Although Buganda has had many rulers, only those from a royal lineage called Abateregga, which takes its name from Kabaka (King) Kateregga (r. ca. 1614–44), bear the title *kabaka* (pl. *bakabaka*) and occupy the kingship throne, *Nnamulondo*. Thirty-six successive *bakabaka* from this lineage have ruled the kingdom, and their leadership has seen three interregna.[9] This book discusses thirteen of the thirty-six rulers (see figure P.3).

Odhiambo, Ouso, and Williams show that Buganda grew significantly in the fourteenth and fifteenth centuries, and by the eighteenth and early nineteenth centuries it had expanded to include areas of Bunyoro Kingdom. Buganda's location on the northern shores of Lake Victoria (called Nalubaale in Luganda) allowed for its rise to power as the strongest kingdom in the region. Fertile soil supported agriculture and food production that spurred a rapid growth in the kingdom's population. Weak rivals and her ability to absorb foreign influences from European and Middle Eastern cultures also contributed to the kingdom's development. With the infiltration of Arab traders and European explorers, missionaries, and administrators in the nineteenth century, the Baganda developed new skills that enhanced and complemented local practices, including

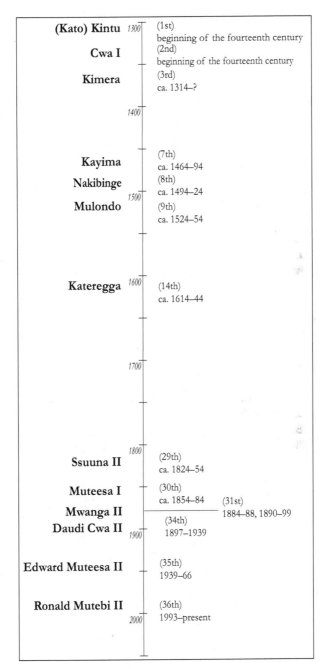

(Kato) Kintu 1300	(1st) beginning of the fourteenth century	
Cwa I	(2nd) beginning of the fourteenth century	
Kimera	(3rd) ca. 1314–?	
1400		
Kayima	(7th) ca. 1464–94	
Nakibinge	(8th) ca. 1494–24	
1500 **Mulondo**	(9th) ca. 1524–54	
Kateregga 1600	(14th) ca. 1614–44	
1700		
1800 **Ssuuna II**	(29th) ca. 1824–54	
Muteesa I	(30th) ca. 1854–84	(31st) 1884–88, 1890–99
Mwanga II **Daudi Cwa II** 1900	(34th) 1897–1939	
Edward Muteesa II	(35th) 1939–66	
Ronald Mutebi II 2000	(36th) 1993–present	

Figure P.3. Kings and reigns discussed in this book.

bark-cloth manufacturing, elaborate reed-palace and reed-fence building, ironworking, and special wooden canoe building. Moreover, the highly centralized government system that Buganda had developed under the *kabaka* "gave a sense of continuity and prestige that kept alive [his subjects'] loyalty and patriotism."[10]

Arab traders facilitated the introduction of Islam, which took a strong hold in the nineteenth century, as the historian Kevin Ward writes. Islam was followed by Christianity, to which Baganda had "remarkable adaptability and receptivity."[11] The first missionaries to arrive in Buganda were representatives of the Anglican Church Missionary Society (CMS). They arrived at the court of Muteesa I (r. ca. 1854–84) on June 30, 1877, followed by several Pères Blancs, White Fathers, who were French Catholics, on February 17, 1879. Islam and Christianity competed for devotees, alongside other foreign and local religions, with Protestantism and Catholicism as common rivals.[12] Missionization laid the groundwork for colonial rule.

When Uganda became a British protectorate in 1894, British administrators immediately instituted indirect rule through Buganda's *kabaka* and his chiefs. Central to this agenda was the Uganda Agreement of 1900, which gave the kingdom "special status" within the Protectorate of Uganda and "recognised the 'traditional' institutions of Buganda, including the monarchy and the territorial chiefs appointed by the Kabaka [*kabaka*]."[13] Citing Apolo Kagwa, "the most influential Ganda [Kiganda] intellectual in the first two decades of the twentieth century," the historian Neil Kodesh astutely points out that "Lakes royal officials exploited the circumstances of colonial rule to present a particular vision of the precolonial past."[14] Indeed, "The 1900 Agreement held great symbolic meaning for Baganda, in terms . . . of [both] national pride and the prestige attach[ed] to the monarchy."[15]

Between 1900 and the 1950s, conflicts arose between colonial administrators and the Buganda government. One such conflict was the desire of Sir Andrew Cohen, the governor of the British Protectorate of Uganda, "to integrate Buganda much more closely into the structures of Uganda, so that Uganda as a whole could develop towards greater responsibility and gradual self-government."[16] This desire led Cohen to arrest and exile Kabaka Edward Walugembe Muteesa II (r. 1939–66) to London in 1953.[17] The furor the exiling of the king raised among Baganda compelled Cohen to bring Kabaka Muteesa II from Britain back to Uganda in 1955.[18] For the nearly two years the *kabaka* was in exile, Buganda's complex sociopolitical hierarchy was destabilized. In other words, the kingdom was out of tune.

Buganda experienced debilitating political instability during the postcolonial era. When Uganda acquired political independence from Britain in 1962, Kabaka Edward Muteesa II of Buganda became the country's first president. Soon, conflict arose between the Uganda People's Congress Party of his executive prime minister, Apollo Milton Obote, and the conservative Kabaka Yekka (King Alone) movement and party. In 1966, the conflict led Obote to order the national army, under the command of General Idi Amin, to attack Kabaka Muteesa II's main palace (*lubiri*) in Mmengo. This attack prompted Kabaka Muteesa II to go into exile in Britain in 1966, where he lived until his death in 1969. In 1967, the Ugandan government adopted a new constitution that made Obote president and terminated both the federal system and the country's kingdoms. This development led to the demise of Buganda, for there was no reigning *kabaka* for almost three decades.

According to the anthropologist Ben Ray, in 1971 Idi Amin, Uganda's president from 1971 to 1979, facilitated the return of Kabaka Muteesa II's body to Uganda as a way of garnering Buganda's support for the 1971 coup d'état that made him president.[19] Amin needed the backing of the Baganda, as they were the largest and most politically influential population in the country.[20] The Baganda welcomed Amin as a liberator from Obote, although they never forgot the attack he had led on Muteesa II's palace. The return of the *kabaka*'s body from Britain gave them hope for restoring their monarchy. In fact, the Baganda were able to install Kabaka Muteesa II's son, Prince Ronald Mutebi II, as his successor.[21] However, it soon became clear that Amin never had any intention of reinstating the monarchy. His government prevented Mutebi II from completing the rituals that would signify the prince's enthronement and the restoration of the Kiganda kingship.[22] The prince's coronation never took place.

In 1979, the Tanzanian government overthrew Amin. Yusuf Kironde Lule, a Muganda and the leader of the Uganda National Liberation Front, became Uganda's third president. However, a vote of no confidence led to his resignation within a few months after he had taken office. Godfrey Lukongwa Binaisa, also a Muganda and a former attorney general of Uganda, succeeded Lule and ruled for about one year. He left office after the Military Commission arrested him on charges of mismanagement of office. The commission and its chairman, Paul Muwanga (also a Muganda) held the powers of the president until late 1980, when Uganda held its first elections. Obote retook the presidential office after his Uganda People's Congress won the elections. However, Major General Bazilio Olara-Okello overthrew him in 1985.

In 1981, the current president of Uganda, Yoweri Kaguta Museveni, began organizing an intense military campaign against Obote's government. As part of that campaign, which was based in Buganda, Museveni formed the National Resistance Movement Party and the National Resistance Army. Using the forces of the National Resistance Army, he seized power in 1986.[23] In 1993, his government politically restored all formerly abolished kingdoms, allowing for the enthronement of the current *kabaka*, Ronald Mutebi II. It is important to point out that the government never restored the federal system that had been established by the 1900 Agreement. This system had helped sustain many elements of Buganda's precolonial nation-state identity, and had given the kingdom much autonomy during the colonial and part of the postcolonial periods.

Twenty-first-century Buganda, then, is generally a kingdom with less of its original political power, most of which rests with the central government of Uganda. However, the Baganda recognize the *kabaka* as their leader and the apex of Buganda's sociopolitical hierarchy, which, again, is grounded in the intertwined institutions of kinship, clanship, and kingship. These institutions and the hierarchy they support serve as the core of the politics discussed in this book. An important aspect of political life in Buganda is the different counties (*masaza*) into which the Baganda have historically divided themselves—currently there are eighteen.[24] The Baganda are divided into sects on the basis of their permanent residence in these counties, including Bannabuddu (residents of Buddu County), Bannakyaddondwa (residents of Kyaddondo County), and Bannabusiro (residents of Busiro County). These sections continue to be an important feature of sociopolitical organization in the kingdom that Kawuugulu tunes.

Introduction

Kawuugulu Musical Performance, Politics, and Storytelling

Kiganda Politics and Kawuugulu Musical Performance

The Baganda are organized into over fifty patrilineal clans (*bika*, sing. *kika*). These clans are exogamous in the sense that members marry outside of their clans. Each clan traces its origins to a forefather called *jjajja w'ekika*, "grandfather of the clan," who may not have been one of the clan's original leaders. Also, every clan has a leader called *mukulu w'ekika*, "head of the clan"; in addition, every clan head has a unique title name. Clan heads run an administrative structure that all clans share. The structure comprises different hierarchical levels (see figure I.1), each of which contains several lineages of people, with independent leaders.

These lineages allow clan members to manage their growing numbers. For instance, when the population of a clan level grows large enough to require multiple leaders, its members may approach the clan head to request approval to create one or more additional lineages. Because the Baganda are a patrilineal group, they have primary membership in their fathers' clans and secondary membership in their mothers' or matrilineal clans. Many people, however, acquire secondary membership in clans through blood brotherhood (*mukago*), marriage (*bufumbo*), or kinship between ancestors of different clans. Every clan has a primary totem (*muziro*) and a secondary totem (*kabbiro*). A totem may be a plant, an animal, a part of either one, or a nonliving substance such as water from a special source or an inanimate object such as an awl (*lukato*). Clans take their names from their primary totems. It is taboo to eat a totemic animal and plant, consume a totemic substance, or use a totemic object, in part because many consider totems as kin. Clans discussed in this book include those with an animal as the primary totem and those with a plant as the primary totem:

Clans with an Animal as Primary Totem
Ffumbe (Civet Cat) Clan
Lugave (Pangolin) Clan
Mbogo (Buffalo) Clan
Mmamba (Lungfish) Clan
Mpeewo (Oribi) Clan
Ndiga (Sheep) Clan
Ngabi (Bushbuck) Clan
Ngeye (Colobus Monkey) Clan
Ngo (Leopard) Clan
Njovu (Elephant) Clan
Nkima (Monkey) Clan
Nkula (Rhinoceros) Clan
Nvubu (Hippopotamus) Clan

Clans with a Plant as Primary Totem
Butiko (Mushroom) Clan
Kkobe (Air Potato) Clan
Nvuma (Water Caltrop Seed) Clan

The *kabaka* is the head and unifier of all clans. Historically, most *bakabaka* have taken wives from many different clans to strengthen the loyalty of those clans. However, the current *kabaka* and his wife have chosen to be monogamous. Unlike most Baganda, *bakabaka* trace descent through their matrilineal lines, and therefore they have primary membership in their mothers' clans. These clans have historically ensured greater safety for them than their patrilineal clans when conflict and violence (such as rivalry for the kingship throne), have arisen among princes.[1]

Every clan has at least one official hereditary duty to perform for the *kabaka*. Clan members enact these duties within his main palace or royal enclosure (*lubiri*) and within the wider kingdom. Stressing the role these responsibilities play in strengthening and sustaining clan-royal ties, the Butiko (Mushroom) Clan member Anthony Mugagga Muwagga, who was born in 1966, noted that the clan responsible for making and preparing the *kabaka*'s bark cloth (*mbugo*) protects knowledge of this work from nonprimary members of the clan. This clan never lets non-clan individuals touch the fabric, partly fearing that its primary members might lose their special connection to the *kabaka*.[2]

The Butiko Clan is in charge of entertaining the *kabaka* and protecting him from invisible malevolent spirits. Clan members accomplish these duties through Kawuugulu performances.[3] The performers protect the *kabaka* when he is on foot during a procession. Through a ritual known as *okutabaala kabaka*, literally, "waging war for the king," they serve as his security guards and detectives. Kawuugulu clan apexes (*busolya*, sing. *kasolya*, literally, "roof") headed by *aboobusolya* (sing. *owaakasolya*)

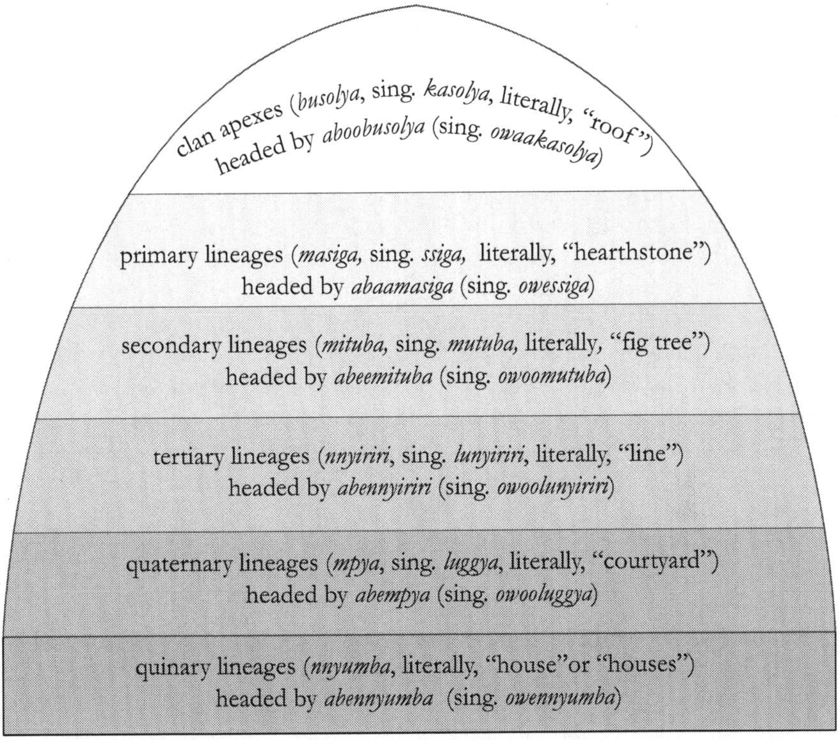

primary lineages (*masiga*, sing. *ssiga*, literally, "hearthstone") headed by *abaamasiga* (sing. *owessiga*)

secondary lineages (*mituba*, sing. *mutuba*, literally, "fig tree") headed by *abeemituba* (sing. *owoomutuba*)

tertiary lineages (*nnyiriri*, sing. *lunyiriri*, literally, "line") headed by *abennyiriri* (sing. *owoolunyiriri*)

quaternary lineages (*mpya*, sing. *luggya*, literally, "courtyard") headed by *abempya* (sing. *owooluggya*)

quinary lineages (*nnyumba*, literally, "house" or "houses") headed by *abennyumba* (sing. *owennyumba*)

Figure I.1. Clan administrative structure of Buganda.

members go ahead of the *kabaka* and his royal entourages to identify and clear away any problems they may detect, including malevolent spirits or sorcery.

Since the primary members of the clan, Aboobutiko, have hereditary ownership over the ensemble, they are its principal performers. However, they permit some secondary members of the clan to perform with them, particularly individuals with whom they have close kinship or blood ties through marriage and blood brotherhood, among other kinds of connections. Eligible performers include Abengeye, primary members of the Ngeye (Colobus Monkey) Clan. This group performs because the ancestors of Aboobutiko and Abengeye engaged in blood brotherhood and marriages that allowed their descendants to become close relatives. Similarly, Abenvuma, primary members of the Nvuma (Water Caltrop Seed) Clan, are eligible performers in Kawuugulu on the basis of once having been clanmates with Aboobutiko. Bakaaboobutiko, wives of Butiko clansmen, can also perform after bearing children. Butiko clanwomen's children, *bajjwa*, are also eligible performers because of the close ties they have with the clan via their mothers. These arrangements (discussed in greater detail in chapter 4) demonstrate the relatively flexible nature of

Kiganda consanguinity. Such flexibility makes it possible for Kawuugulu performances to bring together and manage many different clans and members of different affiliations, classes, statuses, genders, and faiths.

Aboobutiko guard Kawuugulu from primary members of other clans with the help of the ensemble's invisible supernatural power (for more detail on this, see chapter 1). They may open their performances by requesting that people who are unsure of their close kinship with the clan refrain from singing and dancing to Kawuugulu drums. Ensemble members stress the drums' ability to punish ineligible performers who dare to perform with them. Primary members of other clans acknowledge and respect Kawuugulu's power partially because they guard their respective royal duties in similar ways. The agency of Kawuugulu, particularly that of the ensemble's drums, marks it as distinct from many other Kiganda ensembles, and sets them apart as uniquely associated with special prerogatives: entertaining and protecting the *kabaka*. The drums enable the ensemble to act as a moral force with the exclusive right to adjudicate proper conduct.[4] Moreover, Kawuugulu's association with the *kabaka*, who oversees all clans, is a large part of what makes the Butiko Clan so important. While other clans serve the *kabaka*, none of their duties are as intimate or sustained as Aboobutiko's and their Kawuugulu Ensemble. Therefore, the clan and ensemble have special privileges.

As John Miller Chernoff's ethnography on African drumming shows, similar phenomena are common in many African societies. He writes, "In many African tribes, different social groups have rights and privileges with respect to different types of songs. People organize themselves into musical associations and clubs. In the cities these groups are important not only as embodiments of tribal loyalties and continuities but often as organizations for political and economic action; in the villages, creative effort in musical competitions becomes a way of discriminating status, obligations, and identity."[5] Similarly, Joseph S. Kaminski's study of the Asante *ntahera* trumpets of Ghana shows that performances on these trumpets are a prerogative exclusively of chiefs, as the society restricts such musical events to contexts involving Akan chiefs (not to be confused with kings).[6] Also, Jaco Kruger has observed that bamboo pipe dance (*tshikona*) performances of the Venda people of South Africa "mostly take place under the auspices of traditional leaders, and they are associated with important social rituals."[7]

In the case of the Butiko Clan of Buganda, its use of Kawuugulu performances to entertain and protect the *kabaka* dramatizes the "rights and privileges" of all other clans by underscoring that the *kabaka* is the head of all the clans and that they all serve under his authority. Through standing in for other clans, Aboobutiko (Butiko Clan members) and their Kawuugulu performances articulate various principles of kinship, clanship, and kingship (figure I.2).[8] This is primarily how the Butiko Clan and its ensemble help sustain the hierarchy that interweaves kin and clan ties in delicate tension with royal prerogatives,

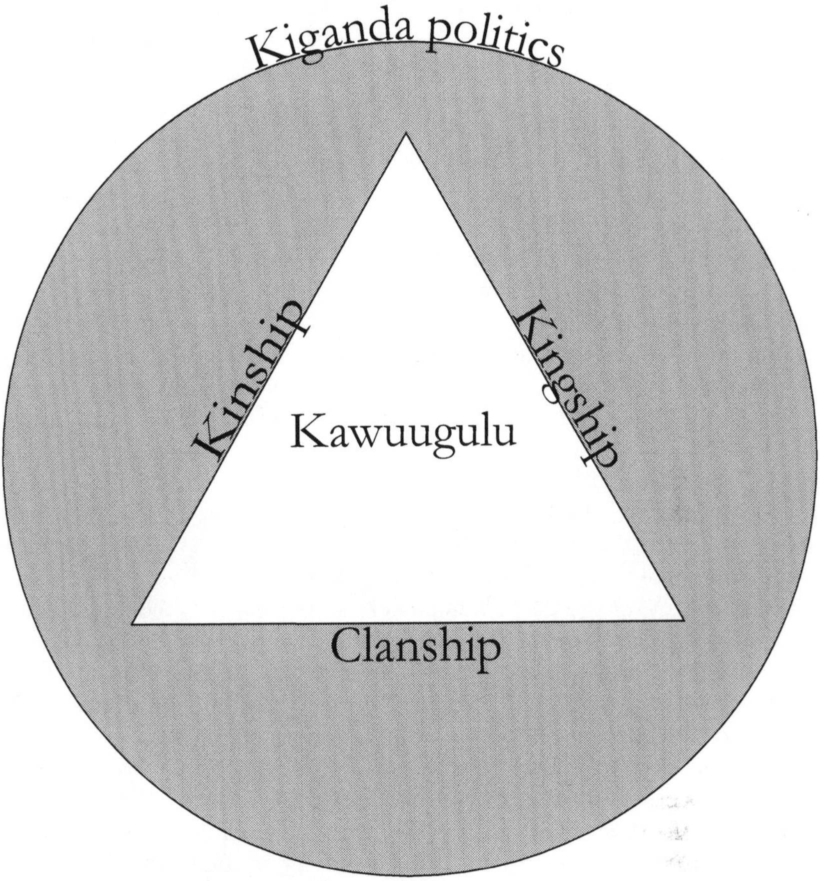

Figure I.2. Kawuugulu and Kiganda politics.

in this way tuning the Kingdom of Buganda. As a result of their encompassing nature, Aboobutiko and Kawuugulu unite various clans explicitly, and all clans implicitly. In so doing, they create a sociopolitical contract that remains alive as long as the ensemble performs. Just as Kawuugulu performances create bonds among its members, Aboobutiko dictate the fulfillment of social responsibilities between the *kabaka* and all clans.

Storytelling and Kawuugulu Musical Performance

The primary source of Kawuugulu's political potency is a body of oral stories that inform its performance practice.[9] These stories document how and when the ensemble grew in relation to Buganda's changing circumstances, providing a record of the adaptability of both institutions. The stories bolster political and moral legitimacy and act as a framework for articulating and reinforcing principles of politics. Furthermore, they determine Kawuugulu's sound and performance structure (the sequence of drumbeats, songs, and dance movements), context (when and where the ensemble performs), and the various practices associated with the ensemble's musical instruments and non-musical performance paraphernalia.

Keith Howard astutely writes that "musical practice is accorded value through nuanced interpretations of history."[10] This observation is particularly relevant to Kawuugulu's history, which is archived in stories that are diverse. For the ensemble, "nuanced interpretations" of its oral narratives should take into account their multiple origins and treat different versions of a single story as separate stories.[11] Every use or capacity of Kawuugulu items has its unique origin, and therefore needs its own explanation. Like historical events, these items have inspired different accounts, each saying something unique about the ensemble. Thus, the value of Kawuugulu oral accounts lies in their differences, not in their uniformity. The tellers of the stories have not eliminated divergent accounts for centuries, therefore I do not. Nor do I present these stories as contradictory; after all, the tellers do not see the accounts as culturally conflicting. The diversity of Kawuugulu's oral accounts enriches its narrative, for no single story can contain all the various aspects of the ensemble. This diversity reflects the ensemble's multifaceted cultural significance, which, again, involves Aboobutiko and their Kawuugulu Ensemble representing multiple clans before the *kabaka*. Variations among these stories testify to the dissimilar perspectives at play in Kiganda sociopolitical life, which both the *kabaka* and clan leaders must keep in mind if they are to collaborate smoothly. Because competing claims about Kawuugulu are tantamount to competing claims about the Kingdom of Buganda, again, we should not assume there is one correct story. Part of the political currency of the ensemble's oral accounts lies in their multiple means of interpretation and ability to encompass many accounts, just as Kawuugulu performances bring together multiple, contrasting drumbeats, songs, dance movements, and non-musical practices. It is this diversity that allows the stories to bolster the historical legitimacy of Kawuugulu performers, enabling them to posit certain moral qualifications of what defines legitimate forms of rule, in particular, appropriate interactions between the *kabaka* and the clans he oversees. The complementarity of the various oral narratives stresses these forms of interaction.

However, Kawuugulu stories are not just oral but also performative. The ensemble's multiple performance contexts are forms of stories. Ensemble members mainly perform at official or social Butiko Clan events, which often take place in the homes of clan leaders and elders. According to my research in the late 2000s, these events include child initiations and confirmations (*okwalula abaana*), twin initiations (*okwalula abalongo*), weddings (*embaga*), final funeral rites (*okwabya olumbe*), and installations of leaders (*okussaako abakulembeze*). The ensemble's performances also accompany recitations of genealogies of the clan's various lineages (*okulanya*) and events in which Aboobutiko get to know each other better (*okumanyagana*). These events are common across the various clans of Buganda. Therefore, Aboobutiko's integration of Kawuugulu into the occasions highlights the ensemble's broader importance and relevance to the Kiganda domains of kinship, clanship, and kingship. Ensemble performances in these contexts articulate the very means by which Buganda and its society manage themselves. Kawuugulu also performs at Aboobutiko's development seminars, fundraisers, and graduation celebrations. These newer performance contexts highlight and reflect the ensemble's adaptability to cultural change.

Given Kawuugulu's role in entertaining and protecting the *kabaka*, the ensemble is an integral feature of royal occasions that involve him. These include official ceremonies and celebrations of the *kabaka*'s birthday, coronation, and wedding anniversaries. Kawuugulu performs in royal contexts without the *kabaka* only on rare occasions. According to Pius Sempa Kawere, a Kawuugulu performer who was born in 1929, in 1955 ensemble members performed to celebrate the potential return of Ssekabaka Muteesa II (r. 1939–66) from exile, after he had been exiled by Governor Andrew Cohen in 1953. Immediately following the *kabaka*'s exile, clan heads (*bataka*) across Buganda took a stand and took the case to court. On the day testimony for the prosecution took place, the verdict clarified that Cohen had wrongly assumed the right to exile Muteesa II, according to Section 6 of the Uganda Agreement of 1900. As soon as Aboobutiko learned about the verdict, they transported Kawuugulu instruments to Bulange, Buganda's administrative building and headquarters, and later to the *kabaka*'s main palace in Mmengo to join in celebratory performances.[12] The clan's use of Kawuugulu as a mechanism for resistance and affirmation was unusual. During the abolition of Buganda, from 1967 to 1993, the monarchy had lacked a reigning *kabaka*. As a result, Kawuugulu's royal performances were largely inactive during that time. Since the Butiko Clan's revival of these performances in the early 1990s, they are minimal. Bulasio Katimbo, a Kawuugulu performer who was born in 1958, and tertiary lineage head (*owoolunyiriri*) in the Butiko Clan, noted that today the *kabaka* may travel across the kingdom or appear in public without being accompanied by ensemble members.[13] Consequently, his government rarely remunerates the performers with cows as it did before 1967, according to Hannington Joshua Kizza Mugwanya, a Kawuugulu performer born in 1956.[14] These practices and arrangements are symptoms of a weakened kingdom, with less political power, most of which rests with the central government of Uganda.

Kawuugulu drums also narrate stories. The users of these drums consider them and treat them as kin, kings, and ancestors or spirits. Historically, the drums have personal names and a private house. Kawuugulu members feed, dress, and make requests to them. Because these drums have life and supernatural qualities, they speak as well as sing like their human players. With the aid of these players, Kawuugulu drums communicate specific messages, evoking the Luganda saying *Ndi ŋŋoma, njogera matume* ("I am a drum, I speak that which I have been sent to speak"), and its variation *Ndi ŋŋoma, nseka matume* ("I am a drum, I laugh the way I have been instructed to laugh"). The drums' beats and their associated texts as well as the songs and dances that accompany them tell stories. So does their symbolism and that of other forms of performance paraphernalia featured in the larger Kawuugulu Ensemble. Like the oral narratives that inform its practice, the stories that Kawuugulu performance contexts and drums as well as other forms of paraphernalia tell have diverse sociopolitical meanings.

Because Kawuugulu "actors" include more than the human performers, the ensemble integrates many different human and non-human stories (figure I.3). I use Ruth Finnegan's term "multimodal" as a collective descriptor for these stories; multimodal, too, is the politics these stories shape, which in turn involves kin, clans, and the *kabaka*.[15] This multimodality, in conjunction with the agency of Kawuugulu drums, allows the ensemble to mediate different forces, including male and female, visible and invisible, living and dead, relatives and ancestors, royals and commoners, primary and secondary, present and past, as well as wakefulness and sleeping.

Studying Kawuugulu

Despite my ties to Kawuugulu, I never attended the ensemble's events as a child or teenager. When I was growing up in the 1980s and 1990s, Buganda lacked a reigning *kabaka*, rendering Kawuugulu inactive. However, I learned about the ensemble through stories from my maternal relatives, Aboobutiko. My music and dance performance teachers at Buganda Road Primary School introduced me to the popularized version of Kawuugulu dances known as Amaggunju. Other students and I performed the dances during school, regional, and national competitions and festivities held to showcase Uganda's cultural heritage. I later learned from a relative that anonymous teachers had attempted to introduce and teach Amaggunju dance movements at academic institutions starting sometime in the mid- or late twentieth century. According to the source, this practice became more widespread during the abolition of Uganda's kingdoms from 1967 to 1993. Concerned about the misrepresentation associated with teaching their dances in academic contexts, Aboobutiko tried to stop the practice.

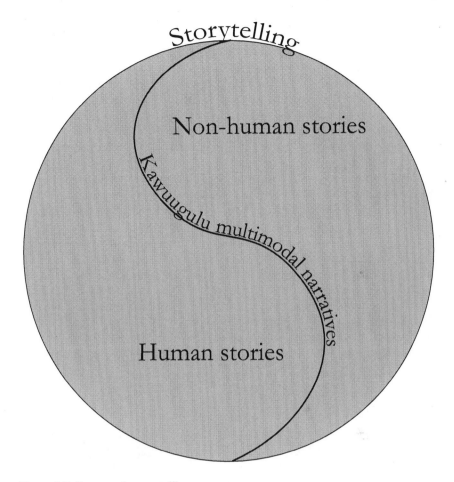

Figure I.3. Kawuugulu storytelling.

However, tracking down the teachers responsible for disseminating the practice was practically impossible, as Aboobutiko struggled with reinforcing proper Amaggunju etiquette during this time. Schoolteachers continued presenting modified versions of the dances' formations and their accompanying musical repertoire.[16] Such forms of "invented tradition" are still common today, and one should not confuse them with official Kawuugulu dance performances in clan and royal contexts.[17]

In the early 1990s, following the restoration of formerly abolished Ugandan kingdoms, Aboobutiko revived Kawuugulu events. After watching televised performances of the ensemble in royal contexts, I developed an interest in studying the history and practice of Kawuugulu. As an undergraduate at

Makerere University in the early years of the twenty-first century and, later in the decade, as a new graduate student in the Musicology Program at Florida State University, I considered conducting an ethnomusicological study of Kawuugulu. However, such a study was not feasible due to limited resources and restricted access to the ensemble. I instead researched a Kiganda royal bow-harp called *nnanga* and the *kabaka*'s royal musicians.[18] These projects augmented my understanding of the relationship between musical practice and sociopolitical hierarchy in Buganda.

In the fall of 2007, after about a year during which I discussed the possibility of investigating Kawuugulu with Aboobutiko, clan leaders voiced official approval for my research. I conducted the initial fieldwork from the summer of 2008 through the fall of 2010, and additional fieldwork in the summers of 2012, 2013, 2014, and fall of 2015. The investigation took me to dozens of villages and towns across Buganda. I primarily gathered information about Kawuugulu and Kiganda politics through structured and unstructured interviews, which I combined with participant observation and secondary research. This book is the culmination of these activities in the various locations I worked.

The contributions of my interviewees to this project varied depending on experience, age, status, clan affiliation, and the topics we discussed. Throughout the book, I provide brief biographical information about these interviewees to contextualize their connections to, and views about, Kawuugulu or its links to politics in Buganda (more detailed information on the interviewees is provided in appendix B).

Conversations with Aboobutiko

As mentioned earlier, Aboobutiko have historically closed off and closely guarded information about Kawuugulu, making it inaccessible to outsiders. Consequently, knowledge of the ensemble is not widespread even among ordinary Baganda. A few secondary members of the Butiko Clan are knowledgeable about Kawuugulu, but the preponderance of the information I discuss in this book came from Aboobutiko, especially those who are interested in maintaining the Kawuugulu Ensemble's historical practices.

I identified potential Aboobutiko interviewees primarily through recommendations. For instance, many Aboobutiko and Kawuugulu performers recommended talking to my late maternal granduncle Kabenge Gombe (figure I.4) because of his extensive knowledge of the ensemble.

Kabenge Gombe, who lived from 1931 to 2016, was cited as one of a few surviving authorities on Kawuugulu's historical practices. Mike Kasirye, born in 1942, noted that Gombe was teaching him and other Aboobutiko historical information about the ensemble that he had acquired from his father, and other deceased clan elders (*bakadde*).[19] Fredrick Kaggwa Semugooma, born in

Figure I.4. Kabenge Gombe (*center*) playing the *Nyoolaevvubuka* drum.

1951, described Gombe as a guardian of secret and sacred information about Kawuugulu.[20] Muhammad Sensonga, an elder and head of a primary lineage (*owessiga*) in the Butiko Clan who was knowledgeable about the ensemble— also a Kawuugulu performer born in 1928—acknowledged that Gombe's knowledge surpassed his.[21] Like many other interviewees, George William Kalyemenya, a performer born in 1940, referred me to Gombe as a better source of answers to my questions.[22]

Clan elders seemed more informed about the ensemble than younger members, as was confirmed by my encounter with Goreti Nalugunju, also a Kawuugulu performer who was born in 1982. Nalugunju advised me to consult with her father, a clan elder, about the details regarding the materials used to make the original Kawuugulu drum set. When I inquired why she was unable to answer many of my questions, she noted that clan elders were the preeminent guardians of this information. She told me that at one point she had listened in on one of her father's conversations with a group of clan elders. The elders had previously met in her father's home to discuss clan matters, including Kawuugulu. During their meeting, she heard them mention that Aboobutiko's ancestors had extracted the initial beaters of the ensemble's drums out of human hands.[23] Nalugunju's indirect access to her father's knowledge highlighted how the Baganda stress patrilineality over matrilineality, and how this arrangement is reflected in the transmission of Kawuugulu knowledge among Aboobutiko. These interactions and testimonies confirmed that although the clan owns

Kawuugulu, knowledge of the ensemble's existence and practices vary from individual to individual, family to family, and lineage to lineage. This is why in this work, views of some interlocutors might feature more prominently than others.

Kabenge Gombe

My first formal interview with Gombe about Kawuugulu confirmed many of his clanmates' views about his knowledge and experiences. He admitted that he had learned a great deal about the ensemble from his father—my maternal great-grandfather, Petero Mukasa Kabuzi (1882–1983), who was a Kawuugulu performer and a custodian of Butiko Clan history. He oversaw numerous clan duties in the *kabaka*'s main palace, and mentored various Butiko Clan heads (*baggunju*), including Kamiiri, the twenty-second clan head (*ggunju*); Pantaleo Dibya, the twenty-third; Experito Balinnya, the twenty-fourth; and Matia Kawere, the twenty-fifth and current clan head.

Gombe recounted how, as a child, he had regularly escorted Kabuzi to official functions at the principal clan estate (*butaka*) in Bukalango and to the *kabaka*'s palace in Mmengo. Gombe would observe his father's performances and keenly listen to his conversations with clan elders at these functions. In the mid-1930s, Gombe temporarily lived with his maternal uncle Erasto Mugwanya, who resided at Lubya, close to the *kabaka*'s palace. Gombe's proximity to the palace compelled him to make frequent visits there to observe and learn about Kawuugulu performances in royal contexts. Due to meager financial resources, he started formal schooling at age ten. His time at home—coupled with his curiosity, desire to learn new things, and exceptional memory—gave him various opportunities to learn from Kabuzi about Kawuugulu and Kiganda politics, mainly through listening to stories and asking questions.

In 1948, Michael Bazzebulala Nsimbi, a well-respected historian of Kiganda culture, visited Gombe's father to inquire about Aboobutiko in order to include information about them and their clan in a book he was writing on Kiganda names and their origins.[24] Gombe offered to assist Kabuzi in looking through his documents to find important information, such as dates, that Nsimbi would find relevant. This gesture prompted Nsimbi to solicit Gombe's assistance in carrying out further inquiries about Aboobutiko within Kyaggwe County, where Gombe and his father lived. Nsimbi compensated Gombe and Kabuzi for their assistance by purchasing them a new bicycle. He also gave them a stipend that could help pay Gombe's school fees for a lengthy period. This experience catalyzed Gombe's love for research, leading him to write many unpublished works that are largely based on the wealth of information he acquired from Butiko Clan elders.[25] Since passing away in 2016, Gombe's close relatives have secured this work in his home in Namirembe, and hopefully they will publish it as an edited collection in both Luganda and English.

Gombe held notable positions, including serving as a Kabaka Foundation official; consultant with the Luganda Language Association, president of the Luganda Authors' Association, and secretary of Volunteer Promoters of Church Music. Moreover, as already pointed out, within the Butiko Clan Gombe served as a deputy primary lineage head (*owessiga omusigire*), secondary lineage head (*owoomutuba*), Kawuugulu instructor, and performer who sang and played the *Nyamitongo* and *Nyoolaevvubuka* drums with a high level of proficiency. His experiences as a performer, educator, historian, linguist, consultant, and administrator made him a unique participant in this project, and I was truly honored when he agreed to serve as my principal research assistant.

Gombe's knowledge and experiences significantly contributed to my ability to analyze the complex relationship between Kawuugulu and political life in Buganda; it would have been impossible to undertake this project without his generous support. He and I first discussed the project during the summer of 2006 when I was completing my master's degree in musicology at Florida State. During that summer I traveled to Uganda for my betrothal and wedding ceremonies. Gombe served as one of the main speakers at the betrothal, or pre-wedding introduction ceremony, helping my fiancée to formally introduce me to her family in Kitengeesa, Makasa District (figure I.5). During his speech, he briefly highlighted the value of my previous research on the royal music institution of Buganda and its contribution to ongoing efforts in preserving undocumented Kiganda musical practices (figure I.6). Present at the ceremony was a former *katikkiro*, prime minister, of Buganda, Joseph Mulwanyammuli Ssemwogerere, who took note of Gombe's remarks about my work. When it was the *katikkiro*'s turn to speak, he commended and encouraged me to study other Kiganda royal, musical practices that had received little documentation (figure I.7). By this time I had learned of the threat that modernity was posing to Kawuugulu practices. This knowledge, along with the *katikkiro*'s encouragement, inspired me to engage in a lengthy discussion about documenting Kawuugulu as part of my doctoral research. Gombe welcomed the idea, helping me to formulate the initial research proposal that we shared with the current *ggunju*, the Butiko Clan head, Matia Kawere.

Gombe further mobilized support for the proposal among other clan leaders and elders. During my fieldwork he played a key role in encouraging many of my Aboobutiko interviewees to participate in the research that informs this book. Also, he introduced me to knowledgeable research participants within and beyond the clan, helped me to articulate my research questions, advised me on how to remunerate interlocutors for their time, scheduled and coordinated interviews on my behalf, assisted with negotiating difficult situations, and escorted me to interviewees' homes. Gombe's presence at many of the interviews made it easier for Aboobutiko to be forthcoming and at ease, because he was a well-respected clan administrator and elder. May Gombe's soul rest in eternal peace.

Figure I.5. Author (*center*) being received by his fiancée's paternal aunts at the couple's betrothal, or introduction, ceremony in Kitengeesa in 2006.

Figure I.6. Gombe (*right*) introducing author to his fiancée's family in Kitengeesa in 2006.

Figure I.7. Former Buganda Katikkiro (Prime Minister) Joseph Mulwanyammuli Ssemwogerere (*right*) speaking at the couple's betrothal, or introduction, ceremony in Kitengeesa in 2006.

Beyond Butiko Clan Precincts

To supplement perspectives of Aboobutiko with those of other Baganda, I interviewed primary members of different clans about Kawuugulu and Kiganda politics. These individuals included performers, linguists, historians, and drum makers. Interviewing makers of ordinary and ritual drums at Akugoba Drum Makers and Mbogo Drum Producers in Mpambire, and Sikyomu Drum Makers in Nateete, allowed me to better contextualize Kawuugulu drums within the broader domain of Kiganda drums (figure I.8). Similarly, including the perspectives of spirit mediums (*bakongozzi*) of deceased kings (*bassekabaka*, sing. *ssekabaka*) directly connected to Kawuugulu enabled me to understand the ensemble's ties to Kiganda royalty.[26] I interviewed the mediums of Ssekabaka Nakibinge (r. ca. 1494–1524) in Bubinge-Mitweebiri, Ssekabaka Mulondo (r. ca. 1524–54) in Bulondo-Mitweebiri, and Ssekabaka Kateregga (r. ca. 1614–44) in Buteregga-Mitweebiri. These individuals are also the caretakers (*balabirizi*) of the tombs of the *bassekabaka* whom they serve as mediums (figures I.9, I.10, and I.11). My conversations with custodians of Buganda's main palace in Mmengo and the tombs of Ssekabaka Muteesa I, Ssekabaka Mwanga II (r. 1884–88, 1890–99), Ssekabaka Cwa II (r. 1897–1939), and Ssekabaka Muteesa II (r. 1939–66) in Kasubi also informed my views on Kiganda

Figure I.8. Sikyomu Drum Makers' workshop in Nateete.

Figure I.9. Author and the spirit medium of Ssekabaka Nakibinge (*right*), standing outside the *ssekabaka*'s tomb in Bubinge-Mitweebiri.

Figure I.10. Ssekabaka Mulondo's tomb in Bulondo-Mitweebiri.

Figure I.11. Ssekabaka Kateregga's tomb in Buteregga-Mitweebiri.

Figure I.12. The tombs of Bassekabaka Muteesa I, Mwanga II, Cwa II, and Muteesa II in Kasubi.

kingship (see figure I.12). Information coming from outside the Butiko Clan generally allowed for a better contextualization of Kawuugulu's historical and political importance in Buganda.

The Politics of Fieldwork on Kawuugulu

There was a lot of politics involved in researching Kawuugulu, and the process called for a negotiation of my different identities. Most of my interactions with mediums of *bassekabaka* and custodians (*balabirizi*) of their tombs did not go smoothly. Some mediums refused to allow audio or video recording, or even photography, and others never opened up. A few were forthcoming and at ease only when I revealed particular identities or affiliations. A medium who requested anonymity expressed discomfort with recording, filming, and photographing him, wondering why I wanted to tape information that historically has been transmitted orally. He also expressed concerns about the way I would handle the information I wanted him to share. According to the medium, I was too young and lived too far away (outside Uganda) to be trusted as a faithful gatekeeper of such information. Without disputing his views, I tried to explain that recording our interview would enable me to play it back in the future for analytical purposes, and that I would not publish any information he shared with me against his will. This explanation never satisfied his concerns, so we agreed that I would take a few notes instead of recording.

Similarly, when I first interviewed the medium of Ssekabaka Nakibinge and caretaker of his tomb (*ssiro*) about Kawuugulu, he avoided answering any of my questions. He stated that it was his responsibility to guard information about the ensemble from outsiders. However, when he learned that I was a clanswoman's child in the Butiko Clan, he graciously agreed to talk about the ensemble. The medium asked me not to record his voice, though, a request I respected. He also instructed me to first put some monetary alms in a basket that was in front of him, an act he described as *okugula eŋŋoma*, "buying a drum." The medium explained that the alms would please Ssekabaka Nakibinge's spirit, causing it to possess the interlocutor so that he could answer my questions. I was uncomfortable with the idea of spirit evocation, but I complied with the medium's request in order to acquire information to which only he might have had access. As soon as he was under spirit possession, he narrated various stories, including one about Ssekabaka Nakibinge's ties to the *Kawawa* royal spear featured in Kawuugulu events.

At the conclusion of the medium's narration, he advised me to approach Aboobutiko directly with further questions about Kawuugulu. He stressed that they would agree to answer the questions since the group grants its clanswomen's children absolute access to the traditions and practices of the ensemble. Confirming that the clan would let me participate in Kawuugulu performances, he further stressed that I was free to join in without fearing harm from the ensemble's drums, although the instruments would kill or incapacitate individuals without what he described as *omusaayi gw'ekika* ("clan blood") who participated in Kawuugulu musical events.[27] Several mediums asked me not to publish some of the fascinating stories they recounted; I would not have had access to those stories without negotiating my identities as a Muganda, relative, scholar, multilingual researcher, student, teacher, performer, and Christian, among others. Such negotiation ultimately allowed me to collect sufficient information for this book.

From a Clanswoman's Child to a Researcher

In her discussion of fieldwork, Sylvia A. Nannyonga-Tamusuza has defined the field as "a dialogical space for research where people interact with the aim of understanding themselves and others better and then . . . communicate this knowledge to a wider audience."[28] This definition captures and reflects some of the dynamics I investigated in Buganda, where kinship structures political and musical relationships. Because Kawuugulu's practice lives in people and their relationships to one another, I had to live and understand the relationships the ensemble engenders and inhabits. Accordingly, studying Kawuugulu necessitated a process of self-reflection to understand better who I was in relation to the people I was studying.

I am a primary member of the Ndiga (Sheep) Clan, which is my patrilineal clan. My secondary, matrilineal clan is Butiko. Given the "analogic" nature of Kiganda kinship, most of my research participants, especially Aboobutiko, were close or extended family relatives. I borrow the term "analogic" from Roy Wagner's discussion of the Diribi people's kinship system. Wagner describes "analogic kinship" as regarding "kin relationships" and "the relatives identified through those relationships . . . as basically alike in some important way."[29] As expressed by the saying *Ebukojja teva wa lubu lwo; buli avaayo aba nnyoko* ("From one's maternal side comes no sibling; everyone from there is your mother"), every primary member of the Butiko Clan was my "mother." Consequently, Aboobutiko addressed me as a *mujjwa*, "clanswoman's child" or "sister's child," reminding me that I was related to them although I was not part of the clan's patriline. I was neither accountable to the patriclan's jural obligations nor entitled to its privileges, and yet I still belonged.

The Baganda believe that *bajjwa* (sing. *mujjwa*) have a supernatural power that allows them to neutralize spells, dispel unseen problems, and dismiss consequences of breaking cultural rules within clans that regard them as *bajjwa*. This belief is the basis of the saying *Omujjwa y'amala ebibamba*, "It is a clanswoman's or sister's child who averts misfortunes or calamities." Aboobutiko's *bajjwa* are eligible performers in Kawuugulu because of their "blood" ties to the clan through their mothers. Also, their ability to avert misfortunes grants them special access to Kawuugulu performances, through which Aboobutiko claim their *bajjwa* solve the clan's social problems. I grew up aware of the ways clans revere their *bajjwa*. However, my research gave me a fresh experience of the social power they have in Buganda.

Various interviewees commented on my status as a *mujjwa* in the Butiko Clan. Deziderio Kiwanuka Matovu, a Ngabi (Bushbuck) Clan member and tube-fiddle (*ndingidi*) player who lived from 1924 to 2015, told me that if I put one of my hands in an empty pouch belonging to my maternal uncle, his money would fly away like the wind, and eventually run out. In order to prevent this loss, he would have to put some cash in the pouch before I placed my hand inside, and I would be entitled to that money. Matovu added that if a primary member of the Butiko Clan were to hang himself, as a *mujjwa* I am one of the people the clan would call upon to cut the victim off the rope, rather than a primary member of the clan.[30] Similar remarks came from many Aboobutiko themselves, most of whom encouraged me to take part in Kawuugulu events in hopes that such contexts would provide appropriate opportunities for me to break spells in their lives. Although I am unsure I met their expectations, this power dynamic underpinned my participation in the ensemble's performances and access to important information about it.

Unsurprisingly, my position as a *mujjwa* among Aboobutiko made me a figure Victor Turner would describe as "liminal."[31] Turner writes, "The attributes of liminality or of liminal *personae* ('threshold people') are necessarily ambiguous, since this condition and these persons elude or slip through the network of classifications that normally locate states and positions in cultural space. Liminal entities are neither here nor there; they are betwixt and between the positions assigned and arrayed by law, custom, convention, and ceremonial."[32] According to Peter Kinene, a primary member of the Lugave (Pangolin) Clan born in 1969, I was not a "true child" of the Butiko Clan. The clan valued me because of my ability to eliminate some of its problems. This was a "filthy job" that the clan would only assign to an outsider. A Butiko Clan's relative through blood brotherhood (*mukago*) was closer to its primary members than I was.[33] As these statements demonstrate, it is the *bajjwa*'s "liminality" that perhaps allows them to mediate between secret, internal knowledge and the public, outside world.[34] They have "power" in their mothers' clans because they are "outsiders," and this power can affect "insiders" in significant ways. In my case, the power allowed for a deeper understanding of Kawuugulu. Additionally, my distance helped me make sense of the web of relationships in which I found myself entangled. I both belonged to and was excluded from the Butiko Clan, analogous to the relationship between Kiganda clans and Kawuugulu performances.

My status in the Butiko Clan also mirrored the relationship of Kawuugulu to Kiganda kingship. In another interview with Matovu, he suggested that the clan's duty of ensuring the *kabaka*'s safety through the ensemble's performances has historically earned Aboobutiko the status of Buganda's "analogic" *bajjwa*. According to the interlocutor, when the group performs on Kawuugulu drums at occasions involving the *kabaka*, it exterminates all misfortunes and problems that would have harmed him, a responsibility similar to *bajjwa*'s in every clan in Buganda. The spirits that possess the performers whenever they beat the drums and dance to their drumbeats help guard Buganda's leader when ensemble members perform ahead of him in procession.[35] By protecting and entertaining the *kabaka*, Aboobutiko and their ensemble—both of which represent but are distinguished from all other clans—clean out the kingdom as *bajjwa* can do for their mothers' patrilines. Kawuugulu can perform this duty because of its "liminality," in the same way I gained access to many historically guarded stories about the ensemble because of my "liminal," insider-outsider status in the clan. This status, and my particular subject position, enabled me to maintain a healthy balance between personal ties and academic research.

Certainly, my kin ties with many of my research participants played a central role in the documentation of their life stories and the ways they intersect with those of Kawuugulu. Making kinship dynamics the heart of my ethnography was a fluid and messy approach that made me feel vulnerable at times. However, it has allowed for a comprehensive understanding of Kawuugulu and better expression of my interlocutors' voices. These voices and mine—as well as our shared identity—are the foundation of this book's narrative.

Participant Observation

My observation of and participation in Kawuugulu events as a drummer have made it easier for me to analyze the ensemble's connections to Kiganda political life and to transcribe Kawuugulu repertoire (figure I.13). In June 2008, for instance, I was involved in two events featuring the ensemble at the home of the current *ggunju*, Butiko Clan head, Matia Kawere, in Lugala (see figures I.14 and I.15). One of the events was a betrothal, or pre-wedding introduction, ceremony during which the *ggunju*'s daughter introduced her prospective husband to her family for their approval. The other event was a training workshop in which officials from the Kabaka Foundation addressed Aboobutiko about clan-based philanthropy and community development. The following month I participated in the performance that led Kabaka Ronald Mutebi II (1993–present) to the Buganda Parliament building grounds in Mmengo, where he received King Mswati of Swaziland. Participating in Kawuugulu's clan and royal performance contexts made me more knowledgeable about the ensemble's role in articulating and embodying principles of Kiganda kinship, clanship, and kingship. Unfortunately, I was unable to record or photograph many performances in royal contexts due to security concerns. Similarly, Aboobutiko requested me not to record many performances in clan contexts, due to their personal nature, and many of the clan's administrators asked me never to teach Kawuugulu music and dance repertoire to non-members of the clan.

Secondary Research

I carried out secondary research at a number of institutions, including the Uganda Society and Uganda Museum in Kamwokya; Ggaba National Seminary in Ggaba; Kyambogo University in Kyambogo; Makerere University in Makerere; Uganda National Cultural Center in Nakesero; and Central Broadcasting Services in Mmengo. Some of the historical literature at these institutions has informed my discussion of different aspects of Kiganda history,[36] clanship,[37] kingship,[38] and government.[39] The perspectives featured in these sources have also informed my analysis of ethnomusicological literature that discusses different aspects of Kiganda politics in relation to musical practice.[40] A contact at Central Broadcasting Services shared video recordings of Kawuugulu performances from the 1993 coronation and inauguration, as well as the 1999 royal wedding of Kabaka Mutebi II. These recordings informed my analysis of Kawuugulu performances in royal contexts.

Figure I.13. Author (*right*) playing the *Nyoolaevvubuka* drum.

Figure I.14. Kawuugulu performers rehearsing in the home of the *ggunju*, the Butiko Clan head, in Lugala.

Figure I.15. Ggunju Matia Kawere (*left*) at his daughter's betrothal, or pre-wedding introduction, ceremony in Lugala.

Closing Remarks

This project offers historically and ethnographically informed perspectives on Kawuugulu and its political importance. Given the centrality of storytelling to the project, I use stories as the foundation of the book's theoretical framework and analytical apparatus, both of which primarily draw on local views. Similarly, I use storytelling to present and analyze multiple narratives about Kawuugulu's ability to "tune" the Kingdom of Buganda. For readability and clarity, I have kept text in the Luganda language to a minimum. I generally present a trans-lated narrative—what Claude Lévi-Strauss described as "cooked" rather than "raw."[41] Chapter 1 introduces contemporary Kawuugulu and its practice. Chapters 2, 3, and 4 discuss the relevance of the ensemble's musical perfor-mance and storytelling to intra-clan, inter-clan, and royal politics. In chapter 5 I draw on a single Kawuugulu event to theorize the ensemble's integration of musical performance, politics, and storytelling.

Chapter One

The Kawuugulu Clan-Royal Music and Dance Ensemble

The Kawuugulu Clan-Royal Music and Dance Ensemble is commonly known by one of the collective names of its dances, Amaggunju. A rough translation of Amaggunju is "dances associated with the *ggunju*," an interpretation that highlights the Butiko Clan leader's, the *ggunju*'s, historical duty of overseeing Kawuugulu's performance practice and facilitating its development. The ensemble's official name, Kawuugulu, is mainly used by Aboobutiko and serves as a cover term for all aspects of Kawuugulu practice: sound and non-sound instruments, drumbeats, songs, dances, performers, and stories.

The name originally belongs to one of Kawuugulu's two twin principal drums, *Kawuugulu*. A diminutive form of the Luganda word for "owl," *kiwuugulu*, the drum name *Kawuugulu* confirms Alan Merriam's observation that some musical instruments are "harbingers of certain kinds of messages of general import to the society at large."[1] In Buganda, an owl's cry is a bad omen and portends disaster, particularly death.[2] Accordingly, the ensemble name Kawuugulu highlights Aboobutiko's association with the *kabaka*'s, king's, spiritual life and Kawuugulu's responsibility to warn of potential danger ahead of his processions.

Before the 1966 attack by the central government on the Kingdom of Buganda's main palace (*lubiri*) and the 1967 abolishment of all Ugandan kingdoms, Kawuugulu was one of many performing groups that served the *kabaka*.[3] The attackers killed many of the performers in these groups and destroyed important musical instruments, but Kawuugulu survived partly because it never resided permanently in the palace. Since the revival of the ensemble's royal performances in the early 1990s, it is one of two active Kiganda royal musical ensembles, the second one being the Mujaguzo Drums of Kingship. This chapter introduces Kawuugulu with a focus on its political agency in twentieth- and twenty-first-century Buganda and the impact of missionization, colonialism, and postcolonial conflict on its practice during these eras.

The Ensemble Drum Set and Performance Paraphernalia

The core of Kawuugulu is a set of six drums. As we shall see in the following chapters, these drums have a hierarchy, each drum or drum pair has a unique history, and each drum's name has a specific meaning that highlights its history. The Kawuugulu drum set is incomplete without a royal spear known as *Kawawa*, which serves as a marker of the Kawuugulu Ensemble's royal status. This spear has a large, oval bronze blade attached to a long, wooden shaft that performers shove into the ground, upright, and among ensemble drums when they perform (fig. 1.1).

Kawuugulu's six drums include the ensemble's two main drums, *Kawuugulu* and *Kasajja*. The player of these drums performs while standing, striking their membranes with wooden drumsticks and releasing them instantly. The player produces two main open tones that serve as the foundation of the drum pair's beats, or musical offering. The interval between the two drums' tones is approximately a fourth. This pair has wooden shells that are roughly hollow—open at the top and bottom—conical, and slightly narrower at the top (see fig. 1.1). Cowhides cover the top and bottom of each drum's shell, held in place with cow leather cords. Bark cloths, *mbugo* (sing. *lubugo*) adorn the bodies of the two drums. This fabric is significant among the Baganda. They have historically used it for clothing and securing or marking items of great value such as jaw bones of a deceased king.[4] In fact, Kawuugulu performers place all the ensemble's items on a large bark cloth to mark its special royal status (see fig. 1.1).

The ensemble also includes a pair of small drums, called *Nyamitongo* or *Namitongo*, whose shapes and designs are similar to those of *Kawuugulu* and *Kasajja* (fig. 1.1). *Nyamitongo's* player performs on his knees to honor the drum pair's association with Ssekabaka Mulondo (r. ca. 1524–54) and, similar to *Kawuugulu* and *Kasajja's* player, uses two wooden beaters to produce open tones on the two drums. *Nyamitongo's* tones are approximately an interval of a third apart, and the drum pair's player plays ostinato-like patterns that add depth to Kawuugulu music throughout the performance.

Kawuugulu's fifth drum is *Nyoolaevvubuka*. The drum's player performs while standing, with his instrument between his legs, leaning its head against the edge of the *Kawuugulu* drum. Beating the instrument with his palm at the center of the drumhead, he plays a hollow, deep tone. He also produces a high-pitched tone by hitting the area close to the edge of the membrane with the tips of the index, middle, ring, and little fingers of either hand. The drum's two tones are an interval of about a ninth apart. *Nyoolaevvubuka* has a wooden, hollow, conical shell with a wider cup-shaped head and a narrower base and a monitor lizard (*nswaswa*) skin covers the top of the drum's head (fig. 1.1). Wooden pegs fasten the skin to the shell.

Figure 1.1. Set of Kawuugulu instruments: *Mpuunyi*, *Kasajja*, *Kawuugulu*, and *Nyoolaevvubuka* drums (*back row, from left to right*); *Kawawa* royal spear (*center*); alms basket, *Nyamitongo* drum pair, and beer gourds.

Figure 1.2. The *Kijoboje* drum.

A medium-sized drum named *mpuunyi*, which appears similar to the drum pairs mentioned above, is Kawuugulu's sixth drum (fig. 1.1). The player of this drum, similar to the *Nyamitongo* drummer, performs while kneeling. He produces a deep, open tone by hitting the area close to the edge of the drumhead with one palm as his second hand supports the drum. The name *mpuunyi* is universal, referring to the drum that establishes and maintains the central beat of music in most Kiganda ensembles. This drum also regulates performance tempo and controls the timing of dancers as they transfer their weight from one foot to the other during the dance. *Mpuunyi* means "hummer" or "moaner," suggesting the ability of Kawuugulu drums to sound like their human players. Kawuugulu members may replace the *mpuunyi* with the Butiko Clan's identity drum, *Kijoboje*, which a single drummer plays with two heavy wooden beaters while standing (see fig. 1.2).

When performing, Kawuugulu members are often dressed in white, loose-fitting tunics called *kkanzu*, made from silk, cotton, poplin, or linen. The tunics are a more recent addition to the ensemble; according to the oral historian Kafeero Mukasa (b. 1971), Arab traders introduced them in Buganda during the reign of Ssekabaka Ssuuna II (r. ca. 1824–54).[5] Like many people in precolonial Buganda, Kawuugulu performers historically wore animal hides (*maliba*) and bark cloths. Dancers cinch their tunics around their waists with colobus monkey (*ngeye*) fur belts called *bikuzzi* (see fig. 1.3). The dancers attach cotton strings to the ends of the belts and use these strings to fasten these belts around their waists. The performers also tie metallic pellet bells (*ndege*) around their ankles with the aid of twisted sheep leather cords or laces called *ndere* (see fig. 1.4). All these costumes serve as signifiers of specific principles of kinship, clanship, and kingship.

Kawuugulu dancers address each other as Ababinyi—"Raisers" or "Jumpers"—and describe the style of their dance movements as Okubina, which involves jumping and lifting or raising legs very high. According to many ensemble members, these terms differentiate Kawuugulu dancers and their performance style from others in Buganda.

Drum Classification

Kawuugulu drums fall under a category of ritual drums called *eŋŋoma ez'ensonga*, literally, "reasoned drums" or "purposed drums." The process of making and tuning these drums is unique because it involves consultation with special sages called *bagezi*. The sages may recommend what items to place inside the drum shells before drum makers and tuners, *baleezi*, stretch hides over them. These items reflect the drums' purposes, which in turn determine the creation and tuning of the instruments. The makers and tuners of *eŋŋoma ez'ensonga*

Figure 1.3. Kawuugulu dancers wearing colobus monkey fur belts for dancing over white tunics.

rarely disclose these items, citing the proverb *Akali mu ŋŋoma kamanyibwa muleezi* ("The content of a drum is known by its maker or tuner"). However, the objects rattling around inside the shells of these drums are audible when the musical instruments are moved around. The practice of enclosing items in drum shells in Buganda is also common among makers and tuners of ordinary drums, called *eŋŋoma eza bulijjo*, or *eŋŋoma ez'ebinyumu*: "party drums." However, the items enclosed in these drums, such as pebbles and pieces of wood, are neither secret nor sacred like those in *eŋŋoma ez'ensonga*. Francis Walakira, a maker of *eŋŋoma eza bulijjo* and *eŋŋoma ez'ebinyumu* who was born in 1971, told me that such objects signify the drums' lives.[6]

The sages whom makers and tuners of *eŋŋoma ez'ensonga* consult may also help determine the drums' pitches and may further recommend specific melo-rhythmic patterns with their associated textual phrases (*mibala*) for these drums. These *mibala* vary depending on how the tuners of *eŋŋoma ez'ensonga* tension their heads. Makers and tuners of *eŋŋoma ez'ensonga* also tend to hold a much higher status than that of *eŋŋoma eza bulijjo* and *eŋŋoma ez'ebinyumu* makers and tuners, partly because *eŋŋoma ez'ensonga* help solve social problems and protect people or institutions. In fact, some *eŋŋoma ez'ensonga* makers and tuners tend to compare their status to that of the Kireezi, the official repairer of Kiganda royal drums. The Kireezi has been responsible for various royal

Figure 1.4. Pellet bells that Kawuugulu dancers tie around their ankles laced with cords made of sheepskin.

drums, including the Mujaguzo Royal Drums of Kingship, which affirm the existence of the monarchy and sound at all official ceremonies involving the *kabaka*; the *Vvamuluguudo* ("Get out of the road") drum, which historically accompanied the *kabaka* to warn people to clear his path; the *Njagalakweetikka* ("I want to carry") drum, which Buganda's *katikkiro*, prime minister, traditionally sounded to alert the *kabaka* that he was on his way to serve him; and the drum that the Nkima (Monkey) Clan head, the *mugema*, sounds when performing some of the rites that install a new *kabaka*.[7] The use of *eŋŋoma ez'ensonga* is restricted to serving only purposes that their creators bestow. Using them for other purposes is a form of desecration and is thus a cultural taboo.

The Drums' Supernatural Properties

Kawuugulu drums have supernatural twins and power. In one of my interviews, Omulangira (Prince) Mulondo, who was born in 1953 and serves as the spirit medium of Ssekabaka Mulondo and the custodian of his royal tomb, referred to these counterparts as *eŋŋoma ezeebase*, "the sleeping drums," and the Kawuugulu drum set as *eŋŋoma ezitunula*, "the awake drums." Pointing to the former, Mulondo further explained that this supernatural counterpart had once been housed in one of the shelters in the front yard of Ssekabaka Mulondo's tomb (figs. 1.5 and 1.6).[8]

Some Aboobutiko argued that Kawuugulu's supernatural counterpart had ensured the safety of the ensemble's instruments during the postcolonial wars discussed in the preface. Butiko Clan member Anthony Mugagga Muwagga, who was born in 1966, stated that this counterpart turned against the central government forces that attempted to loot Kawuugulu items and other royal artifacts, forcing them to let go of the items.[9] Maria Luiza Ntudde, a Kawuugulu performer born in 1916, recalled seeing stones and rocks dropping down from the sky and hitting the government forces as they tried to vandalize the royal tomb of Ssekabaka Mulondo. According to her, the forces fled without looking back. Ntudde, then a resident of the Bukalango area where Kawuugulu's traditional house stood, added that the scuffles forced many people in the area to abandon their homes in search of safety. Among those who left were the custodians of Kawuugulu instruments, which they had to leave behind because of their large size. When the survivors returned to Bukalango after the wars, an overgrown anthill had enveloped the instruments and bushes, preventing the fighting troops from seizing them. Aboobutiko retrieved the instruments from the anthill while they were still in good shape.[10] These accounts shed light on the role Kawuugulu's supernatural power might have played in the protection of the ensemble.

Figure 1.5. Rocks in the front yard of Ssekabaka Mulondo's tomb in Bulondo-Mitweebiri; according to the *ssekabaka*'s spirit medium the illustrated rocks represent the supranatural counterparts of Kawuugulu and some other Kiganda royal drums.

Figure 1.6. Ssekabaka Mulondo's spirit medium showing the author a demolished house of Kawuugulu's supernatural counterpart in Bulondo-Mitweebiri.

Other Kawuugulu members believe that the ensemble's supernatural double—coupled with the regal status of the *Kawawa* royal spear discussed earlier—helped ensure the spear's safety during the political turmoil. Gombe noted that when government soldiers camped around Aboobutiko's headquarters in Bukalango, they stumbled upon *Kawawa*, and used its blade to harvest bananas and slaughter goats for food. On leaving the area, the forces took the spear with them, but dropped it in a grove on their way out of Bukalango, where non-members of the Butiko Clan discovered it. They wanted to rescue the spear but were afraid to touch it, given the great respect it had garnered prior to the political chaos. During this time, many acknowledged and honored *Kawawa's* position as an artifact of intrinsic importance to the clan. After the wars, some of these individuals found the spear and attempted to save it from peril by asking Aboobutiko to retrieve it. The clan was mystified to learn that the armed forces had abandoned a rare spear with decorations of different metals and several incisions on its bronze ornament, all of which made it attractive to loot and keep as a souvenir. Many concluded that Kawuugulu's supernatural double had in part ensured *Kawawa's* survival.[11] As this account further demonstrates, Kawuugulu instruments have agency, and Aboobutiko's use of those instruments represents all clans' relationship to the *kabaka* and the Kiganda kingship. Kawuugulu musical performance and storytelling manage, structure, model, and legitimize this relationship.

Some Aboobutiko also told me that the clan relied on Kawuugulu's supernatural power to restore the ensemble after the wars. According to Steven Wagaba—a Butiko Clan elder who was born 1917—during the ensemble's revival in the early 1990s, this power, channeled through ancestral spirits, guided Aboobutiko to identify appropriate materials for reconstructing drums that had been destroyed during the post-independence political turmoil. These materials included cow hides and timber for repairing the *Kawuugulu* and *Kasajja* drum pair, as well as python skin for the membrane of the demolished *Nyoolaevvubuka* drum (fig. 1.7). With the guidance of the consulted spirits, the clan identified these materials from the Ssese Islands in Lake Victoria.[12] Muhammad Sensonga, a head of a primary lineage (*owessiga*) in the Butiko Clan born in 1928, explained that some of the drums' hides came from cows with skins that appeared similar to the ones the drum tuners were replacing. The animals had brilliant-looking brown skins with dark spots, and had never mated. Aboobutiko relied on spiritual guidance to validate the eligibility of the prime tuner, or *omuleezi omukulu*, and to carry out all the necessary rites he oversaw. The clan took a small sample of his blood, deposited it on the cow hides, and then performed rites that imbued the hides with supernatural power. These rites took place on a special hill, where the prime tuner spent at least nine days before stretching the hides over the shells and tensioning them. He and his assistants had to reside at the ritual venue throughout the tuning process, which

Figure 1.7. The *Nyoolaevvubuka* drum that the Butiko Clan replaced in the early 1990s; the designs on the drum head represent those of the python snakeskin that covers the head.

lasted for weeks. Representatives from the various lineages of the Butiko Clan performed many duties that complemented those of the prime tuner. For example, a few women prepared food for all the tuners, but it was taboo for women having their menstrual periods to fulfill this duty. The tuning process required all participants to ensure purity through abstaining from having sex and consuming intoxicants.[13] Maintaining Kawuugulu's agency requires spiritual advice and precautions.

Drums as Living Relatives

Because Kawuugulu drums are considered living entities, ensemble members share beer (*mwenge*) or milk (*mata*) with them, and smear cow ghee (*muzigo*) on their membranes, which are referred to as *maaso* ("faces"). Beer is an important beverage in many Kiganda social and ritual contexts, while many Baganda have historically used ghee as body oil, cooking oil, and medicine. Ensemble members store Kawuugulu's beer in a large gourd called a *kita* (fig. 1.8). The gourd sits atop a banana fiber base or wreath, which holds the gourd in position with the support of banana fiber ropes that performers attach to it. The ensemble also features a small gourd that rests against the large one (fig 1.8).

This gourd serves as a cup from which the performers drink and feed their drums. In the absence of beer, the performers may feed the drums with milk. During Kawuugulu events, ensemble members also ensure that they have some ghee to apply to the drum hides.

Diriisa Kasiga, a Kawuugulu performer born in 1969, told of the ensemble traveling to Masaka District in the early 2000s to perform at an official ceremony attended by the current *kabaka*. When it was time for Kawuugulu members to perform for the *kabaka*, the drummers attempted to play the instruments, but they never sounded. Realizing immediately that the performers had not served the drums beer, Ggunju Keleti, the Butiko Clan head at the time, instructed all of them to pour libations on the drums, smear them with ghee, and then put them under the sun for a while to dry. The drummers did as instructed, and when they played the drums again, they sounded. On another occasion, the instruments stayed silent and the performers never had access to beer. As a result, they fed them with milk, and then smeared their faces with ghee; following this treatment the instruments sounded.[14] The performers never explained to me why milk was a suitable substitute for beer, but they stressed that because the drums are living, feeding and oiling them with these substances ensures that they communicate. Oiling the drums and pouring the aforementioned beverages on them could have allowed their membranes to stretch and produce the desired timbre. Nevertheless, the meanings and significance that Kawuugulu performers attach to this practice say a lot about the human qualities attributed to the drums.

Drums' Embodiment of Ancestral Spirits

Since Kawuugulu drums embody ancestral spirits, sharing beer, milk, and ghee with them is also a way of communicating with those spirits. In particular, participants in Kawuugulu events make offerings to the drums as a form of invocation that allows the instruments to meet the participants' social and personal needs. In fact, pouring beer on the drums is ritually similar to how many Baganda pour libations of beer to their ancestors. During Kawuugulu events, Aboobutiko and individuals with close ties to the clan may offer monetary alms called *bigali* to the drums while requesting blessings or giving thanks to the ancestral spirits that the ensemble may invite. Those making offers deposit these alms in an open, shallow, bowl-shaped basket called *kibbo*, with woven strands called *bika*, literally, "clans" (fig. 1.9). These strands are generally made with fiber from banana leafstalks and a type of herb known as *njulu* (*Marantochloa*). Sometimes the basket holds coffee beans that ensemble members eat during performances (seen in fig. 1.9). The first opportunity to make offers belongs to official Kawuugulu members, then other Aboobutiko,

Figure 1.8. Kawuugulu beer gourds.

Figure 1.9. Kawuugulu alms basket containing coffee beans.

and finally closely related secondary members of the clan. The last category may offer alms with permission from Aboobutiko, just as they need the clan's approval to perform in Kawuugulu. All offerers kneel before the basket when depositing their alms. These procedures not only affirm the hereditary ownership that Aboobutiko have over Kawuugulu but also highlight how perspectives about the ensemble drums' spiritual power and agency help shape political life within the Butiko Clan and beyond. The practices confirm the Kawuugulu Ensemble drums' agency.

Drum Storage and Treatment

Aboobutiko have taken great care to preserve Kawuugulu drums and their relationship to living members of the clan and clan ancestors. Consequently, in the past the clan has stored the instruments in their own private house, *nnyumba* or *nju*. In his description of the shelter at the beginning of the twentieth-century, Gombe noted that it was a well-guarded, grass-thatched house with a door laced with elephant grass. A pair of large, dry, stiff cattle hides with cowry shell, *nsimbi*, designs on their edges covered the house's floor. It was on these hides that Kawuugulu performers placed the bark cloths on which the ensemble drums and the accompanying paraphernalia sat. Aboobutiko covered the instrumental set with another dry, stiff cowhide that protected them from rainwater in case it penetrated the grass roof of their shelter. Treating the drums like people, Aboobutiko regularly smeared them with cow ghee.[15]

An elderly man served as one of the custodians of Kawuugulu's house, opening and closing its door in the same way a royal gatekeeper opened and closed the door to the palace or royal enclosure (*lubiri*) entrance. A second custodian, also an elderly man, kept a fire that provided a veil of smoke over the drums and the protective hides at night. He also maintained the embers of this fire during the day to keep vermin at bay. Each of these custodians oversaw the drums and other items housed by Kawuugulu's shelter for a prescribed time, normally a lunar period. Because he had to stay pure during this period, he abstained from sex, just like individuals who played the drums, particularly on the nights before their performance expeditions. In addition, no menstruating or premenopausal woman could enter Kawuugulu's house.[16]

Many Aboobutiko stated that the evangelism and missionary activity that infiltrated Buganda in the late nineteenth and early twentieth centuries affected the Kawuugulu traditions just described. According to Gombe, leaders of missionary crusades burned the cowhides on which the ensemble's instruments had sat in their shelter, as well as its human arm-bone beater, *Nsigadde*, because they regarded them as satanic. The hides and beater had designs of seed kernels and cowry shells, which many Baganda associate with ancestral spirits; they are used in local religious ritual practices. Along with these items, missionaries burned some of the Mujaguzo Drums of Kingship as well as the *Kyebabona* and *Kikwerudde* drums that Ssekabaka Kimera (r. ca. 1314–?) gave to the Butiko Clan for safekeeping.[17] The physical destruction of these and other items in turn led to the elimination or weakening of some spiritual power, largely resulting from the loss of irreplaceable clan materials. As Muwagga stated, cases where ineligible participants in the ensemble's musical events died or went mad as a result of dancing to its drums have become rare in contemporary times because of Kawuugulu's weakened spiritual power.[18]

Many Christians and Muslims participate in Kawuugulu events and criticize missionaries for having diminished the power of its drums. These performers conceptualize this power as more practical than theological, seeing no contradiction between their faith and the drums' ability to punish violations of their code. Flexibility in relation to Kawuugulu's religious practices shed light on the ensemble's adaptability to social and cultural change. Erasmus Kyagaba Binywera, a Kawuugulu performer born in 1933, said that missionary work also led to a decline in the ensemble's performances that commemorated Aboobutiko's forefather Kyebagaba, or invoked his spirit at the appearance of the new moon. According to the performer, these lost practices helped sustain Kawuugulu's spiritual attributes.[19] Charles Lutaaya Muwaga, a Kawuugulu performer born in 1924, also stated that these practices drew Aboobutiko close to their ancestors, who in turn influenced the ensemble's supernatural power.[20]

Today Kawuugulu drums and their associated performance paraphernalia reside in a modern shelter recently erected behind Ggunju Matia Kawere's residence at Lugala. The drums will stay at the clan leader's home until Aboobutiko have raised enough funds to rebuild Kawuugulu's traditional house at its headquarters in Bukalango (fig. 1.10). Herbert Mulasa Bbirikkadde Musiitwa, a Kawuugulu custodian who was born in 1957, explained that during the guerrilla war through which President Yoweri Kaguta Museveni came to power in 1986, fighting between government soldiers and Museveni's forces resulted in the destruction of the shelter and some of the items it housed. The government soldiers, most of whom were anti-Buganda extremists, also attempted to loot and burn some of the instruments during the conflict, but Aboobutiko were able to save them. The clan then transported the instruments from the damaged shelter to the Lubaga home of a primary clan lineage head (owessiga) called Wilfred Mugwanya Kabuusu, for safekeeping.[21] The clan elder Wagaba added that the clan later moved the instruments to his home, which was very close to Kabuusu's. Wagaba initially sheltered the instruments in his garage, but he had to move them, along with other precious royal artifacts, to an isolated place on his property where the government forces would not see them.[22]

According to Musiitwa, storing Kawuugulu drums in Aboobutiko's homes and moving them from place to place put them at risk. Because there was no one to take care of the drums, mice gnawed their skins. The clan had to replace these skins immediately following the conflict to avoid desecrating the drums further. It was taboo for the drums to reside under the same roof as people, especially married couples or individuals capable of having sex.[23] In the same vein, Sensonga indicated that some non-members of the Butiko Clan collaborated with a few Aboobutiko to steal the drums during the political unrest. However, the ggunju, clan head, retrieved and secured them in a safe location when he learned about the plot.[24] Like many Aboobutiko, Musiitwa is concerned that the instruments' current storage might cause them to exact revenge for all the mistreatment they have received.[25] Despite the debilitating effect the postcolonial conflict had on Buganda and Kawuugulu, Aboobutiko have striven to honor the practices that their ancestors established in relation to the instruments' storage.

Music and Dance Performance

A Kawuugulu event lasts about an hour, depending on its context and purpose. For instance, performances that entertain the kabaka and help safeguard him tend to be more elaborate, and therefore last a little longer. Conversely, performances in clan contexts are often shorter because they are part of larger

Figure 1.10. The unfinished modern house (*nnyumba*) of Kawuugulu at the Butiko Clan estate (*butaka*) in Bukalango.

events involving social activities such as feasting and training new ensemble performers. Kawuugulu performances generally open with a single performer sounding Aboobutiko's official *mubala*, its melo-rhythmic beat with an associated textual phrase, "*Weekirikijje; ggunju ajja*" (ex. 1.1).

Luganda	English
Weekirikijje; ggunju ajja,	Prepare yourself in joyful anticipation; the *ggunju* is coming,
yaaaa . . .	*yaaaa . . .* [expression of affirmation]

Costa Nakyagaba, a Kawuugulu performer born in 1971, told me that this *mubala* instructs Aboobutiko to prepare for the arrival of their leader at Kawuugulu's performance scene. It also signals his status as the clan head and presider over clan events featuring the ensemble.[26] Ignatio Kawere Ganaayaba, a Kawuugulu performer and head of a secondary lineage (*owoomutuba*) in the Butiko Clan, born in 1919, expressed the meaning of the *mubala* somewhat differently. He noted that it confirms the *ggunju*'s presence, which in turn signals to the official members of Kawuugulu that it is time to start performing.[27] These interpretations and meanings confirm how Kawuugulu drums communicate like their human players. Following a performance of Aboobutiko's *mubala*, Kawuugulu members perform three main sections or movements that integrate drumming, singing, and dancing (fig. 1.11). Each of the three

Example 1.1. "Weekirikijje, Ggunju Ajja" (Prepare Yourself in Joyful Anticipation, the *Ggunju* is Coming).

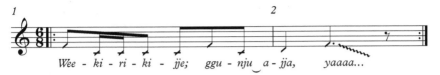

Wee - ki - ri - ki - jje; ggu - nju a - jja, yaaaa...

sections lasts several minutes and each has a unique performance style and tempo (slow, slower, and fast). The performers transition from one section to another with the aid of cues and loud strokes from the main two drums of the ensemble, *Kawuugulu* and *Kasajja*, and these strokes mark the beginnings and ends of the three sections. Although this three-part structure is standard, the sequences of Kawuugulu drumbeats, songs, and dance movements within each section vary from performance to performance. Each ensemble drummer plays a different drumbeat, which complements the rhythmic patterns of other drummers, resulting in a simultaneous layering of multiple drumbeats. The drummers tend to maintain the basic rhythmic formulae of their beats or the variations of those beats throughout the performance. However, the dancers perform several movements within each section, switching from one movement to another with the aid of the principal two drums. The performers' dance formations often correspond to the drum pair's beats.

Similarly, Kawuugulu performs several songs within each section, changing its repertoire depending on cues from the principal two drums. The drumming primarily drives the songs and dance movements. However, the specific order of this repertoire guides the drummers' choices of drumbeats. Within each of the three major sections, the drummers and dancers, many of whom also sing, play complementary performance roles. Only men play drums, but both men and women sing and dance. During performance the dancers often undergo spirit possession.[28] The following chapters discuss the relationship of these practices to kinship, clanship, and kingship.

Kawuugulu's Agency

Clearly, Kawuugulu has agency. Many of my interlocutors regard the ensemble's drums as relatives, ancestors or spirits, and kings. These instruments have emotions and a psychology comparable to those of humans as well as supernatural counterparts. Despite all their power and personhood, however, Kawuugulu instruments need careful guarding, just as powerful persons—including the *kabaka* himself—need protection. Consequently, when the *kabaka* was in exile, the instruments were under threat. They were in some way acting as a double for him. If they vanished or were destroyed, the *kabaka*'s person would probably

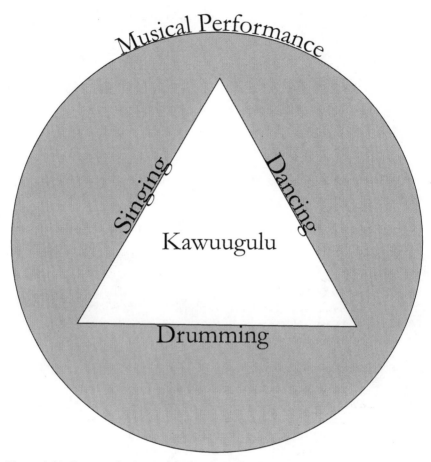

Figure 1.11. Kawuugulu drumming, singing, and dancing.

have diminished in equal proportion. These instruments are irreplaceable, linked directly to the past acts of previous leaders, just as every *kabaka*'s welfare is in some way linked to the soul of a *ssekabaka*, a deceased *kabaka*.

The way Kawuugulu members interact with the ensemble's drums also reflects how the Kiganda political system relies on a delicate balance and relationship between the visible and invisible. For example, the protection of the material (Kawuugulu instruments) allowed the unseen (Ssekabaka Muteesa II in exile) to maintain an extended presence, even beyond the time of his exile. Such ritual practices have concrete effects, so much so that they panicked the postindependence Ugandan government, leading to the 1966 attack on the *kabaka*'s palace in Mmengo and the postcolonial turmoil, which was indeed no small accomplishment.

Chapter Two

Kawuugulu and Intra-Clan Politics

Many Aboobutiko consider Kawuugulu as their twin or double, their *mulongo,* regarding refusal to participate in the ensemble's events as equivalent to disowning the Butiko Clan. To some of these individuals, participation in Kawuugulu events is comparable to birth into the clan and is a confirmation of clan membership, Aboobutiko's identity, and knowledge of the clan's history and practices. To others, the ensemble's instrumental set can punish them if they attend its events and decline to perform with it without a good reason, such as poor health. Punishment for disrespectful behavior can manifest in various ways; some Aboobutiko attest to becoming unsuccessful in their endeavors or subsequently experiencing health problems of some sort. Whatever their social rank, those who attend Kawuugulu events strive to participate in the ensemble's musical performances, formally or informally.

Yozefiina Nakitto, a Ngeye (Colobus Monkey) Clan member born in 1929, recounted that during a performance that facilitated the final funeral rites of a deceased ensemble member in the early 2000s, a Catholic priest took off his robes after leading a Holy Mass and obligingly joined official ensemble members in dancing around Kawuugulu drums. Being a primary member of the Butiko Clan, the priest feared that something bad might happen to him if he refrained from performing. His participation surprised people who expected him to shun Kawuugulu and its practices based on his religious work. The priest's involvement in turn inspired many eligible dancers to get up and dance as well.[1]

This chapter examines how Kawuugulu musical performance and storytelling are inseparable from political life within the Butiko Clan. Focusing on how the ensemble's principal drums, *Kawuugulu* and *Kasajja,* embody, structure, and model this principle of interconnectivity in multiple ways, I argue that different practices associated with these drums help bring various contrasting domains together in a sort of cosmic intersection, allowing Kawuugulu to act as a system of intra-clan politics.

The Origins of Kawuugulu and the Butiko Clan

Existing narratives about Kawuugulu, mostly documented by non-Aboobutiko, indicate that the ensemble emerged when the Butiko Clan made the *Nyamitongo* royal drums for Ssekabaka Mulondo (r. ca. 1524–54).[2] However, according to the accounts of many Aboobutiko, the emergence of the ensemble was an extension of an already-existing musical practice that involved the *Kawuugulu* and *Kasajja* drums. According to an origin story that Kabenge Gombe told me, sometime before the reign of Ssekabaka Kintu, near the beginning of the fourteenth century, a man named Kyebagaba set out to hunt animals in the company of his two sons. However, the three hunters never caught any game. On their way back home they decided to collect firewood and forage for food. While doing this they stumbled upon a thicket filled with small, white, delicate mushrooms, called *butiko*.[3] Kyebagaba and his sons decided to pick the *butiko*. As they were collecting the fungi, a man with whom Kyebagaba was competing for leadership, Wangi Mutizzi, stealthily approached and assaulted him. The victim's two sons ran in panic to inform their relatives and friends about their father's misfortune. On hearing the news, the relatives and friends rushed to the scene in hopes of rescuing Kyebagaba. However, they found neither him nor the bundle of firewood and *butiko* he had been collecting. In order to ease their grief, Kyebagaba's relatives resolved never to eat the *butiko* that had led to the attack on Kyebagaba and his disappearance. Furthermore, the family refrained from eating a creeper plant called *katinvuma*, under which the fungi had been growing at the time of the attack. These events led to the establishment of the Butiko Clan, with the *butiko* serving as the clan's primary totem (*muziro*) and *katinvuma* serving as its secondary totem (*kabbiro*).[4]

When Kyebagaba vanished, his surviving relatives approached a sage called a *mugezi* and expressed to him their grief over the mysterious disappearance of their loved one. The mourners were particularly disturbed by their failure to locate and bury Kyebagaba's remains appropriately. In response, the *mugezi* assured the mourners that supernatural forces had carried the remains to the moon. Before long the grievers saw what they believed to be their deceased relative on the moon, carrying a bundle of firewood on his head. They also saw what looked to them like the *butiko* he had picked before his attack, strewn all over the moon's surface. Now content that Kyebagaba was on the moon, his family followed the *mugezi*'s advice to make twin drums that would commemorate the deceased and the *butiko* that had led to his demise. With the *mugezi*'s guidance, the family identified a tree that had naturally split into two, made a pair of drums from its wood, located Kyebagaba's umbilical cord from where his mother had secured it at the time of his birth, cut it into two pieces, and placed a portion inside each drum's cavity before covering them. This procedure served as Kyebagaba's formal burial.[5]

Figure 2.1. The *Kawuugulu* and *Kasajja* drums paired, with their drumsticks placed on top.

In order to commemorate Kyebagaba's resting place and honor his presence, his family carved a three-quarter moon (*omwezi ogw'eggabogabo*) on the side of each drum when the drum was still very young. The family then tied the twin drums together, encased them in cowhide, covered the ground on which they placed them with additional hide, and designated one of them female and the other, male. The relatives named the female twin *Kawuugulu* ("Small Owl") and the male twin *Kasajja* ("Small Man"), and later used the female drum's name to refer to the set and subsequent additions to it. After making *Kawuugulu* and *Kasajja*, Kyebagaba's family began performing on them during the full moon (*okuboneka kw'omwezi*), yet he had passed away when the moon was at three quarters. Drumming throughout the night, the performers supplemented moonlight with light from elephant grass torches. Kyebagaba's relatives hoped that playing *Kawuugulu* and *Kasajja* as well as singing and dancing to them would compel him to return. They always paired the drums so that they would never be without each other.[6]

Kyebagaba's family also constructed a house where the new twin drums could reside. Moreover, the family initially fashioned a special drumstick, *munyolo*, that completed the drums' twinship. Originally the beater struck only the male drum, but later beat the female one as well. To make the drumstick, Kyebagaba's relatives sacrificed a virgin girl from the lineage of one of his paternal aunts (*bassenga*), and extracted one of the girl's arm bones.[7] They named the drumstick *Nsigadde* ("I have stayed"), after the woman whom they selected to strike the drums. Serving as the hereditary paternal aunt (*ssenga*) of the two drums and all subsequent additions to the set, Nsigadde was responsible for taking care of the drums' shelter. As the meaning of the name Nsigadde suggests, she always stayed behind to guard the house whenever the drums left it for a performance expedition. Her other responsibilities included using the arm-bone drumstick to perform a ritual called *okunaga ku Kasajja*, "striking initial strokes on *Kasajja*, the male drum." Following this initiation, the players of the drums carried them out of their shelter, beginning with *Kawuugulu* (the female drum), followed by the male one, and then the set's accompanying performance paraphernalia. However, the arm-bone beater remained in the drums' shelter, as did its user, Nsigadde. Whenever the drums returned from their performance expedition, their players reversed this order. They carried the female drum ahead of the male one to the compound of their shelter. Here the twin drums' paternal aunt, their *ssenga*, performed another ritual called *okunaga ku Kawuugulu*, "playing initial strokes on *Kawuugulu*, the female drum."

Following this ritual, the players of *Kawuugulu* and *Kasajja* engaged in a welcome-back performance featuring the drum set and its accompanying accessories. The paternal aunt then used the arm-bone beater to perform the final ritual: closing the welcome-back performance by striking cues on the female drum, *Kawuugulu*. After this cue, *Kawuugulu* and *Kasajja*'s players carried the male drum to the pair's shelter, followed by the female drum, and finally the rest of the set's accompanying accessories followed. The twins' paternal aunt had to remain a virgin for the duration of her service, which included overseeing all initiation ritual performances featuring the drums.[8]

Accounts about the origins of *Kawuugulu* and *Kasajja* differ among different Aboobutiko. Matia Kawere, born in 1946, a Kawuugulu performer and the twenty-fifth *ggunju*, Butiko Clan head, stated that instead of using elephant grass torches, Kyebagaba's family supplemented the moonlight with light from a bonfire. The family's all-night performances contributed to other clans' nicknaming Aboobutiko cannibal witches (*basezi*), who are also known to dance at night.[9] The Butiko Clan member Anthony Mugagga Muwagga, born in 1966, also narrated an origin story that offered a slightly different view about the construction of *Kawuugulu* and *Kasajja*'s drumsticks. According to this story, Aboobutiko made separate drumsticks for playing the drum pair during performances that took place beyond its shelter and the property on which the house stood. Moreover, Kyebagaba's family buried the virgin girl in the same hole as they planted the tree that provided wood for making the drums and their drumsticks. This process deified and purified the tree and its wood, allowing the drum pair that the family made from them to acquire otherworldly power. This power had the capacity to punish individuals who defied Kawuugulu performance rules, particularly ineligible performers who attempted to perform with the ensemble. While stretching hides over the drums' shells, Kyebagaba's relatives enclosed in these cavities drumsticks that they made from the bones of the sacrificed virgin's upper arms. Through this procedure the family implanted additional spirits (*misambwa*) in the drums.[10]

These accounts reveal various forms of twinning. The Butiko Clan or Aboobutiko became a sort of twin to Kyebagaba, in the same way that the creeper vine, the clan's initial secondary totem, became its primary totem's twin. Using Kyebagaba's umbilical cord to twin *Kawuugulu* and *Kasajja* highlighted a balance between the visible and invisible, living and deceased, as well as birth and death. Twinning and gendering the drums (male and female) mirrored the doubling of the moon through carving its shape on the drum pair. *Kawuugulu* and *Kasajja*'s paternal aunt, the *ssenga*, memorialized the virgin who died to empower the drums, and the arm-bone drumstick she used became a kind of surrogate twin to the pair, a double of a double. The initial strokes she played on the female drum, *Kawuugulu*, doubled those she played on the male drum, *Kasajja*. Initiating the pair's performances, these strokes doubled those featured in the closing performances. The drums' players also twinned the pair's drumsticks and supernatural power associated with them. These forms of doubling model complementarity in contemporary Kiganda sociopolitical life.

Musical Performance, Storytelling, and Intra-Clan Politics

Some of the musical repertoire that the contemporary Kawuugulu Ensemble performs reinforces the political principle of totemism that the Butiko Clan origin story highlights. The song "Akatiko aka Nnamulondo" (The *Nnamulondo* Mushroom; see ex. 2.1) commemorates a type of mushroom called *nnamulondo*.

	Luganda	English
Call	*Akatiko*	The mushroom
Response	*aka nnamulondo,*	nnamulondo,
Call	*bw'okaggya,*	when you uproot it,
Response	*okaggyira ddala omukonda gwonna,*	you uproot out its entire stem,
	n'ensaanikizo.	and the cap.

These *nnamulondo* currently serve as Aboobutiko's secondary totem, similar to the way the *katinvuma* creeper plant served as the clan's initial secondary totem. Some Aboobutiko suggest that these *nnamulondo* were initially the clan's primary totem, confirming the diversity of narratives about the clan's origins.

Example 2.1. "Akatiko aka Nnamulondo" (The *Nnamulondo* Mushroom).

According to the Kawuugulu drummer Diriisa Kasiga, born in 1969, the phrase *Akatiko aka nnamulondo* encourages Baganda who do not consider *nnamulondo* a clan totem to harvest and eat them. The phrase *okaggyira ddala omukonda gwonna* advises potential consumers of the fungi on how to pick them: uproot them completely without letting their caps become detached from the bases.[11] Kasiga's reference to *nnamulondo*'s caps and bases as "small heads" (*butwe*) and "small feet" (*bugere*) affirms the idea of totems being analogous to relatives in Buganda. In fact, many Baganda hold their totems in high reverence and handle them with great care. Gombe stated that although he never eats *butiko*, he is generally fine with non-Aboobutiko using them for food or in rituals that contribute to sustenance. He added that it would be painful for him to watch people who know that he is a primary member of the Butiko Clan destroying *butiko* without a sound reason or reasonable cause. Such acts would be equivalent to hurting Gombe's relatives and would cause him to question their motives.[12] The Baganda's relationships to each other are analogous to their clan totems' relations to each other. Totems and totemic taboos manage and structure both. Because many people treat totems like people, totem-related taboos are a means of political organization. These taboos also apply to the clans that the totems signify. No wonder most totems are like people.

"Akatiko aka Nnamulondo" also references the female Butiko Clan name, Nnamulondo, indirectly encouraging men associated with Butiko clanswomen to handle them with care, just as many Aboobutiko treat their totems.

Another theme in one of the origin stories presented earlier that Kawuugulu performers sing about is forefatherhood. The song "Abaana ba Kyebagaba" (The Children of Kyebagaba) commemorates Aboobutiko's forefather Kyebagaba, particularly the role his disappearance played in the establishment of the clan (ex. 2.2).

Luganda	English
Abaana ba Kyebagaba,	The children of Kyebagaba,
yaaye!	oh my!
Baalyanga butagaba,	They used to dine without sharing,
yaaye!	oh my!

Ensemble members highlight Kyebagaba's status as a grandfather (*jjajja*) by replacing the phrase *Abaana ba Kyebagaba* with the phrase *Bazzukulu ba Kyebagaba* ("The grandchildren of Kyebagaba"). This practice also serves to acknowledge the existence and importance of the clan forefather figure in Buganda. Participants in Kawuugulu events may interpret the phrase *Baalyanga butagaba* as a metaphorical reference to Aboobutiko's historical responsibility of protecting ancestral practices, particularly those that the Butiko Clan traces back to Kyebagaba.

Some of the musical repertoire associated with the development of *Kawuugulu* and *Kasajja* comments on the leadership of the Butiko Clan head, the *ggunju*. This repertoire includes the three related songs: "Aga Ggunju" (The Dance of the *Ggunju*), illustrated in example 2.3, "Eza Ggunju" (The Ankle Bells of the *Ggunju*), illustrated in example 2.4; and "Aba Ggunju" (The Performers of the *Ggunju*) illustrated in example 2.5. One story about *Kawuugulu* and *Kasajja*'s origin indicates that Aboobutiko developed these songs in honor of the *ggunju*, Butiko Clan head, in the reign of Ssekabaka Kimera, near the beginning of the fourteenth century. During this time, performers on the two drums began entertaining the *ggunju* while continuing to commemorate Kyebagaba. Previously, Aboobutiko had used the term *ggunju* as a name for a pouch that Kasirye, a *ggunju*, made from mongoose (*nkolwa*) hide to hold valuables belonging to Ssekabaka Kimera. However, Aboobutiko's love for the *ggunju*, and desire to please him, compelled them to modify the use of the term, making it an honorific (title) for him.[13] As per historical practice, in contemporary times the three songs just mentioned highlight the *ggunju*'s role in developing Aboobutiko's performances involving *Kawuugulu* and *Kasajja* (and later other ensemble drums), and in overseeing these performances. Accordingly, contemporary Kawuugulu members ensure that he is present at all official ensemble events. Many Aboobutiko told me that in the event of the *ggunju*'s nonattendance, they may use another drum set than the Kawuugulu one. The *ggunju* presides over all clan-related events featuring the official drum set. Accordingly, the set—which honors him—sounds in his presence. Butiko Clan leadership and Kawuugulu performances are inseparable, each depending intimately on the other.

Example 2.2. "Abaana ba Kyebagaba" (The Children of Kyebagaba).

Example 2.3. "Aga Ggunju" (The Dances of the *Ggunju*).

Example 2.4. "Eza Ggunju" (The Ankle Bells of the *Ggunju*).

Example 2.5. "Aba Ggunju" (The Performers of the *Ggunju*).

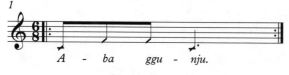

Kawuugulu performers also honor the *ggunju* through the song "Muno omwa Ggunju" (In the Abode of the *Ggunju*), illustrated in example 2.6. The *Kawuugulu* and *Kasajja*'s player often accentuates the rhythmic pattern of this song on the drum pair.

Luganda	English
Asula muno omwa ggunju,	He who dwells here in *ggunju*'s home,
talwa kugejja.	he or she does not take long to fatten.

Portraying the *ggunju*'s home as a constant source of food and comfort, "Muno omwa Ggunju" reinforces his ability to feed Aboobutiko and entices them to visit his home regularly. The song reminds clan members of their leader's hospitality and effectiveness, both of which promote unity and ensure the continuity of the Butiko Clan. "Muno omwa Ggunju" expresses the closeness of the bonds that form in homes through the sharing of food among relations by birth, and among those integrated into the network of dependents that families cultivate through reciprocity. These principles are well documented by the Kiganda saying, *Oluganda kulya; olugenda enjala teludda* ("Kinship is eating; whoever leaves hungry never returns"). If a host offers no food to guests, they might never come back. If he does, they will stay close.

Example 2.6. "Muno omwa Ggunju" (In the Abode of the *Ggunju*).

The song "Abaana ba Ggunju" (The Children of the *Ggunju*), possibly a variation of "Abaana ba Kyebagaba" (The Children of Kyebagaba), discussed earlier and illustrated in example 2.2, also highlights the *ggunju*'s high status and authority. The song's lyrics portray the clan leader as a "father" to Aboobutiko.

Luganda	English
Abaana ba ggunju,	The children of the *ggunju*
yaaye!	oh my!
Baalyanga butagaba,	They used to dine without sharing,
yaaye!	oh my!

Performers may replace the phrase *Abaana ba ggunju* with the phrase *bazzukulu ba ggunju* ("The grandchildren of the *ggunju*") to augment the clan head's authority. Alternatively, they may replace *Abaana ba ggunju* with the phrases *Bwe twabeeranga ewa ggunju* ("When we used to reside at the home of the *ggunju*") or *Bwe twabeeranga omwa ggunju* ("When we used to reside in the house of the *ggunju*"), both of which are reminders of the house's importance as a fundamental unit and model for political relations. The Kiganda proverb *Mu nju temuli kkubo* ("In the house there is no way through") encourages people to welcome strangers and treat them like kin. Through this practice, many Baganda use the house as a model of an encompassing unit that draws others in through various forms of alliance, all grounded in the performance of various kinds of hospitality.

Given the importance of Kawuugulu to political life in the Butiko Clan, Aboobutiko use the songs "Lannama" (Sit with Your Legs Stretched Forward) and its variation (exx. 2.7 and 2.8) as well as "Okulannama" (To Sit with Your Legs Stretched Forward) and its variation (exx. 2.9 and 2.10) to guard the ensemble's musical performances from members of other clans.

Luganda	English
Atudde ku bbali tositama,	You who is seated do not squat,
lanmama!	sit with your legs stretched forward!

*"You" is implied.

Example 2.7. "Lannama" (Sit with Your Legs Stretched Forward).

Example 2.8. "Lannama," variation 1.

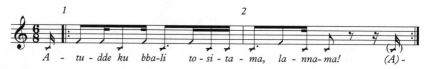

Luganda	English
Oyinze okulannama,	You are able to sit with legs stretched forward,*
nga banaakubba!	It is likely they will rob you!
Tebaakubbe?	Will they not rob you?
Banaakubba!	They will rob you!

* The performers may replace the phrase *Oyinze okulannama* with the phrase *Ozze okulannama* ("You have come to sit with legs stretched forward").

Example 2.9. "Okulannama" (To Sit with Your Legs Stretched Forward).

Luganda	English
Byazze kulannama,	The plump ones came to sit with legs stretched forward
nga banaabibba!	they will probably rob them!
Tebaabibbe?	Will they not rob them?
Banaabibba!	They will rob them!

* The performers may replace the phrase *Byazze kulannama* with the phrase *Byakedde nkya kulannama* ("The dumb ones arose in the morning to sit with legs stretched forward"), *Ggw'okulannama* ("You to sit with legs stretched forward"), or *Otudde okulannama* (You are seated with your legs stretched forward"). Similarly, they may replace the phrase *Nga banaabibba* with the phrase *Oba banaakubba* ("Or it is likely they will rob you").

According to a *Kawuugulu* and *Kasajja* origin story, Aboobutiko often performed on the drums at full moon in commemoration of Kyebagaba. The clan's performances continued from evening until late in the night, attracting many people including individuals with no blood ties to the clan. Sprawled on the well-swept courtyards, these people often got carried away by the excessive excitement of the performances and forgot about their unattended homes. As they watched and enjoyed the performances, Aboobutiko thought of ways to discourage them from attending future performances. Accordingly, the clan created songs about robbing to mock the attendants who had abandoned their homes and left them vulnerable to plunderers and thieves.[14]

Example 2.10. "Okulannama," variation 1.

Complementing this account, the Kawuugulu performer George William Kalyemenya, born in 1940, mentioned that audience members mentioned in the foregoing story actually collapsed from hunger after attending a Kawuugulu performance for days without eating food. Wondering what to do for the starving crowd, Aboobutiko stealthily entered the attendees' homes, snatched their goats, butchered them, and then roasted the meat to feed the spectators. As Aboobutiko prepared the meat for the victims, they performed the songs to mock the attendees. While serving the victims meat from their own animals, Aboobutiko mockingly entertained them with the songs. When the audience returned to their homes, they found their goats missing. It was not long before the victims found out what Aboobutiko had done. As a result, the victims labeled them witches, *balogo*, for their manipulative skills. These experiences also forced the victims to believe that Kawuugulu indeed did have supernatural power that could instantly kill or cause illness in ineligible performers who dared to participate in the ensemble's musical events.[15] In this way, Aboobutiko succeeded at excluding primary members of other clans.

The contemporary Kawuugulu Ensemble uses the songs under examination to request audience members to sit respectfully during its performances. Some Baganda consider sitting with legs stretched forward more respectful than squatting, which might be considered impolite, especially in social settings. But the songs also remind ineligible participants in Kawuugulu musical events not to join the ensemble's performances. Encouraging the audience to sit with legs stretched out could also be an indirect way of denying them access to these performances. The songs additionally suggest the consequences of undesirable participation in Kawuugulu musical events. For example, "robbing" may serve as a metaphor for "killing" or "incapacitating" victims of such ill-advised participation.

Extra-Sonic Performance, Storytelling, and Intra-Clan Politics

To many Aboobutiko, *Kawuugulu* and *Kasajja* are living persons, ancestors, and heirs with a twinned and gendered relationship. Accordingly, Kawuugulu performers dress the drums in bark cloth, exposing only parts of their faces. They ensure that the fabric is intact enough to conceal the drums' nakedness, and to prevent them from getting very cold or sick, just as the players of the drums wear clothing and take care of their bodies. Dressing *Kawuugulu* and *Kasajja*, a reenactment of the historical practice of wrapping the drums in animal hide, highlights the instruments' status as living beings. But Aboobutiko also regard the pair as a representation of the clan ancestor Kyebagaba. This is another reason they wrap bark cloth around the pair, reminding participants in Kawuugulu events of how many Baganda wrap the deceased in the fabric.

Aboobutiko do not see the drums' dual identity as persons and ancestors as a contradiction; to many, ancestors are simply supernatural forces whose existence is taken for granted. Living clan members simply communicate with their ancestors differently than with relatives who are alive.

Interacting with and treating *Kawuugulu* and *Kasajja* as living persons and ancestors highlights the drums' centrality to mediating the visible and invisible domains. Most Baganda believe that the dead never entirely leave the natural world and that they continue influencing the living. Consequently, many people observe appropriate ways of maintaining healthy connections with their deceased relatives. Such conduct may include burying the dead properly (wrapping their bodies in bark cloth, for instance), creating visible monuments that identify them, and visiting as well as maintaining their grave sites. Disrespecting the deceased might cause them to haunt living relatives, or compel them to make certain demands. Such demands tend to include exhuming the remains of the deceased and reburying them suitably.

As the origins of *Kawuugulu* and *Kasajja* and their association with Kyebagaba affirm, appropriate burials are particularly important. Some Baganda believe that it is easier for the deceased to grant the requests of their living relatives if they are happy. Moreover, some of the rituals through which many living Baganda invoke the deceased's spirits traditionally occur at graveyards. The living may request these spirits to deal with individuals who offend some sense of social order, and group requests generally make the appeasement process easier. The living need to treat dead relatives with the same respect they treat their living relatives. When all is said and done, the dead are also alive, though in a different way.

Some interviewees expressed that the *Kawuugulu* and *Kasajja* drum pair is an heir, *musika*. According to Francis Bbirikkade, a Kawuugulu performer and dance trainer born in 1934, Aboobutiko also dress the drums in bark cloth because they are Kyebagaba's *musika*.[16] Some clan members even compare the knotting of the fabric in which they dress the drums to that of the bark cloth that *basika* (pl.) wear on the occasion of their installation. The *musika* is an important figure in Buganda. Following one's death, the family organizes and performs final funeral rites (*okwabya olumbe*) during which members install a *musika* to take over the responsibilities of the deceased. This person must come from the predecessor's clan and is usually a close family member whom the deceased might have selected while still alive. But the family of the deceased may select the *musika* if the deceased never made a will. This *musika* should be capable of honoring the legacy of the deceased, emulating his good qualities, and fulfilling his former responsibilities. Because it is important for all family members of the deceased to know the *musika*, the final funeral rites, during which the family installs him, take place several months following the initial funeral. This allows for enough time to plan the final rites and to announce the date they will take place to all concerned relatives, especially those who might have been unable to attend the burial.

Many Baganda have traditionally not performed these rites or installed *basika* for individuals who have died childless. This practice has encouraged people to have children so that their lineages and legacies can continue, just as the Butiko Clan forefather's legacy continues through his drum pair *musika*. During final funeral rites, an important rite is dressing the *musika* in a special bark cloth. This practice involves a designated person tying the fabric upon the left shoulder of the *musika* in a way that resembles the tying of *Kawuugulu* and *Kasajja*'s bark cloth knots.

Furthermore, the ways *Kawuugulu* and *Kasajja* are transported reflect gender dynamics in Buganda. When transporting the drums, Kawuugulu members load them on a pickup truck, beginning with the male drum and followed by the female drum. Many performers believe that carrying the female drum ahead of the male one desecrates the pair, and may earn the transporters retribution. Gombe explained how a colleague almost lost his life for breaking this rule. The victim was part of a crew that transported *Kawuugulu* and *Kasajja* to the final funeral rites of a Butiko Clan elder from Mubango, Wakiso District, who was a head of a primary clan lineage called Kabanda. The clan transported the drums on different bicycles from the clan estate in Bukalango. On their way to the performance venue, the bicycle belonging to the rider transporting the female drum split in two. The rider fell with such force that his colleagues were amazed he survived. Clan elders who intervened determined that the victim fell because he carried the female drum ahead of the male drum. When the issue was resolved, the victim's colleagues helped him carry the drum behind the male drum to the function venue.[17]

The female drum, *Kawuugulu*, is more honorable than the male drum, *Kasajja*, and because of its noble status, it gives its name to the larger ensemble. Yet, the male drum assumes more authority, which is evident in its role in leading the ensemble during the pair's transportation. Like the male drum, men traditionally command more authority than women. And like the female drum, women command more honor than men. The transportation procedure of *Kawuugulu* and *Kasajja* is a model for and reflection of gender-based hierarchy in Buganda.

Furthermore, the pairing of *Kawuugulu* and *Kasajja* models the complementarity at the heart of sociopolitical hierarchy in Buganda—of male and female genders, natural and supernatural realms, and royal and clan prerogatives—and reflects the notion that every Muganda receives a double at birth, completing the binary nature of procreation (see fig. 2.1). The umbilical cord, *kalira*, represents the double. As one of the *Kawuugulu* and *Kasajja* origin stories reveals, the makers of the drums placed pieces of Kyebagaba's *kalira* in both drums. Traditionally, many Baganda consider a child's *kalira* as his or her double or twin. It ties the child to the clan and family of his father for life and helps ascertain true membership in that clan. According to Gombe, lacking a *kalira* may lead to lacking primary clan membership. A prince may not ascend the throne without his *kalira*, or if it is in a poor state. The officials in charge of the *kabaka*'s coronation often place the prince's *kalira* in a special drum of kingship that he strikes during the enthronement rituals.[18]

I experienced the importance of the *kalira* firsthand during a child initiation and confirmation rite, called *okwalula abaana*, which I observed as a child in the late 1980s. During the event, the paternal grandmother (*jjajja omukazi*), paternal aunts (*bassenga*), and maternal aunts (*bannyina*) of the initiates—who were members of a single family—mixed milk and beer in a tightly woven basket and performed rites that imbued that mixture with invisible power. The initiates' mother (*nnyaabwe*) and some of her sisters then began presenting the candidates to the grandmother along with their *bulira* (pl. of *kalira*). The mother had tied up the *bulira* in a way that made them appear analogous to human heads and feet, to symbolize that they were doubles of their owners. She had also smeared their "heads" with cow ghee, which, as already pointed out, many Baganda use to oil their bodies. In order to affirm the candidates' clan membership, the officiating grandmother submerged each *kalira* into the milk-beer mixture and paused for a moment. Meanwhile, she mentioned that if an initiate's *kalira* emerged from the mixture, the candidate was a true member of the clan and would be confirmed. However, the grandmother would deny membership to any initiate whose *kalira* stayed submerged.

In a previous ritual that I had observed, the officiating grandmother used water that had undergone occult treatment in the place of milk and beer. Similarly, the "heads" of the initiates' *bulira* had to resurface or float in order for the children to receive confirmation. In other words, a resurface of a *kalira*'s "feet" meant disqualification. In both these ritual contexts, participants emphasized that the special treatment of the mixtures by the elders ensured accurate results. Failure to perform the occult treatment of these mixtures, poor storage conditions, or old age of *bulira* may lead to compromised results, leading to chaos. In the first event, an initiate's mother received scoldings from her sisters-in-law, the initiate's paternal aunts, following his unsuccessful initiation. The in-laws accused her of infidelity and bringing "non-clan blood" into their clan through inappropriate means and demanded that she reveal one of the disqualified initiate's real father and clan or else they would ostracize her.

In the second event, everything went smoothly. All initiated children acquired clan names and their new clan retained their *bulira* as confirmation of legitimate membership. This custodianship was the purview of the initiates' paternal aunts. Confirming some of my experiences regarding the importance of *bulira* during the these events, Peter Kinene, a Lugave (Pangolin) Clan member born in 1969, stressed the importance of mothers' ensuring proper preparation, preservation, and protection of their afterbirth. Some families protect and preserve *bulira* by giving them sacred qualities, and their improper handling (such as being touched by a menstruating girl) is taboo and may cause bad luck, disease, or death among family members.[19] Within the Butiko Clan, pairing *Kawuugulu* and *Kasajja*, which allegedly contain pieces of Kyebagaba's *kalira*, is a reminder that Aboobutiko should handle their *bulira*, their doubles, with great care.

Kawuugulu and *Kasajja*'s twinned relationship also highlights the notion of multiple twinning or doubling that permeates various aspects of Kiganda polit- ical life, which the Kyebagaba story illustrates. For instance, a person is born and twinned with his or her *kalira*, but that pair of body and *kalira* are in turn twinned with his or her placenta (*kitanyi*), otherwise referred to as *omwana ow'emabega* ("the rear child"). According to Gombe, the Baganda historically preserved *bitanyi* (pl. of *kitanyi*) of their children with care and secured them under banana plants. They placed boys' *bitanyi* against male banana plants and girls' *bitanyi* against female banana plants. They also placed banana stems around the *bitanyi*. Because of the slippery nature of these stems, they helped deter wild animals from eating the *bitanyi*. Some people even buried deceased relatives close to the locations of their *bitanyi*, and an heir's *kitanyi* could serve as his or her assistant during final funeral rites.[20] Kawuugulu practices mirror and model such forms of multiple twinning, bringing contrasting and comple- mentary domains of Kiganda politics together.

Although the current Kawuugulu lacks a paternal aunt, *ssenga*, who guards its shelter and initiates *Kawuugulu* and *Kasajja* into their performances, the his- torical rituals of the drum pair's *ssenga* (discussed in one of the origin stories presented earlier) model the responsibilities of the *ssenga* in Buganda. Across all clans, before a woman gets married her family assigns her a special *ssenga* who prepares her for a successful marriage and helps her sustain it. The two engage in a number of rituals that nurture decency, creativity, patience, perse- verance, self-control, a work ethic, humility, kindness, cleanliness, and cook- ing skills. The *ssenga* may also help identify an appropriate future husband for her mentee, prepare her for enhanced sexual pleasure with the husband, and introduce him to the young woman's parents and family. Her responsibilities continue into the marriage of the mentee, who is free to share any challenges she encounters with the *ssenga* and ask her for advice. These and other respon- sibilities of the *ssenga* highlight an important kind of twinning. The *ssenga*, like the brother's daughter, marries out of the lineage. She herself has experi- enced what her niece is about to experience, so mediates the experience. Because Kiganda clans are exogamous, the marriage alliances that *bassenga* (pl. of *ssenga*) foster help mediate relations across primary members of the involved clans. This mediation is very similar to the various forms of mediation that Kawuugulu does.

The Kyebagaba story also highlights the importance of names, *mannya*, to Kiganda sociopolitical life, particularly their role as markers of political identity. Like people, *Kawuugulu* and *Kasajja* received personal names. Each clan in Buganda possesses an exclusive pool of names that distinguish its primary members from those of other clans. Clan names are distinct from proverbial names and the names of ancestral gods or spirits, which members of all clans may possess.[21] Historically the practice was that a person assumed membership in the father's clan at birth, but the clan only officially confirmed membership at the naming ceremony, which followed the individual's initiation into the clan. (More recently, however—starting approximately in the early twentieth century—many people acquire primary clan names at birth and secondary clan names at the confirmation of their clan membership, which can take place sometime during their childhood.)

In her 1960 article "The Eastern Lacustrine Bantu (Ganda, Soga)," Margaret Chave Fallers writes, "Once a child was officially named, he could go to clan functions, and not before."[22] Simeo Ssemmambo Sebuwuufu, a Njovu (Elephant) Clan member and player of a seven-to-twenty-one key xylophone (*kadinda*) born in 1959, explained that names are important markers of clan totems and identity. According to Sebuwuufu, before dating and marrying a lady, he would first request to know her clan name. If the name revealed that she is a primary member of the Mmamba (Lungfish) Clan, he would not get involved with her because she would technically be his "mother." Similarly, he would not marry a woman with a Njovu Clan name because she would be his "sister." Yet he might marry a woman with a name of the Nvubu (Hippopotamus) Clan, for the hippopotamus is his secondary clan totem.[23] These arrangements show the inextricable relationship that clans have with their totems and the names attached to them. The relationship helps maintain respectful, collaborative relations among individuals across various clans. *Kawuugulu* and *Kasajja* document and affirm these and related practices. Such arrangements also help people keep track, from what could be called a genetic point of view, of who is too closely related to be married—even absent modern scientific knowledge of genetics per se.

Last, Aboobutiko continue to guard Kawuugulu performances from non-blood relations. At the beginning of one of the ensemble performances I attended during my fieldwork, Najjuka Nabagereka, a Kawuugulu performer born in 1944, mentioned that Kawuugulu drums can eliminate ineligible performers who attempt to dance with the ensemble.[24] Many Aboobutiko attribute the ensemble drums' agency to the supernatural power with which clan ancestors endowed them when they first created them. Their testimonies demonstrate Aboobutiko's efforts to protect Kawuugulu musical events from the intrusion of individuals without blood ties to the clan, as well as the role of ancestors in sustaining this arrangement.

I also recorded similar accounts by non-members and secondary members of the Butiko Clan who expressed fear of dying or falling sick if they perform with Kawuugulu. They insisted that its supernatural power is in part the basis for nicknaming Aboobutiko, primary Kawuugulu performers, witches (*balogo*) and cannibal witches (*basezi*). Deziderio Kiwanuka Matovu, a Ngabi (Bushbuck) Clan member and tube-fiddle player (*mudingidi*) born in 1924, demonstrated the effect of these allegations when he said he believed that he could not survive the wrath of the drums if he dared to dance to them. He immediately added that they would incapacitate or kill him right away.[25]

Aboobutiko's Musical Double

Like most of the other musical instruments and non-musical paraphernalia that belong to Kawuugulu, *Kawuugulu* and *Kasajja* represent, model, and help structure many principles that shape sociopolitical hierarchy in Buganda, especially those that reinforce various forms of doubling and complementarity: kinship, totemism, forefatherhood, personhood, ancestry, heirship, gender, twinship, and leadership. The two drums are more than mere objects: they are twinned persons and ancestors or spirits. Consequently, they have political agency. One story told of a performer whom they struck down and almost killed because he transported the female drum ahead of the male drum. Such practices allow the drum pair to model gender politics and human marriage in Buganda, where men command more authority and women command more honor. Another story told of a Catholic priest who participated in a Kawuugulu musical event in fear of the drums punishing him for not performing with the ensemble, yet he is a Butiko Clan member. Like this priest, many Kawuugulu performers strive to balance their contemporary lifeways with the need to maintain good relations with their clan ancestors. Ensemble events occur in spite of different religious obligations or spiritual world views, which members see as inseparable. Similar to other Kawuugulu drums discussed in the following chapters, *Kawuugulu* and *Kasajja* have the power to debilitate or punish non-eligible participants. Such sanctions, whether realized through visual or oral transmission, maintain a set of hierarchical distinctions crucial to Kiganda sociopolitical life and monarchical legitimacy. The agency of Kawuugulu drums enables the ensemble to keep various forces in balance within the Butiko Clan, maintaining a hierarchy that in turn assures fecundity and productivity. These, among other practices associated with *Kawuugulu* and *Kasajja*, shed light on why Aboobutiko treat the Kawuugulu Ensemble as a double of the clan.

Chapter Three

Kawuugulu and Royal Politics

Aboobutiko have a historical intimate relationship with the *kabaka*. At the heart of this intimacy lies the clan's protective and entertainment obligations to him, duties that Kawuugulu members primarily enact through drumming, singing, and dancing in royal contexts. Aboobutiko's closeness to the *kabaka* is the subject of the song "Waggongolo Omutanda" (Mr. Millipede the Joiner; see ex. 4.3). Many clan members concur that the song acknowledges the *kabaka*'s readiness to lead them (and members of other clans) without their prompting. According to the Kawuugulu performer Charles Lutaaya Muwaga, born in 1924, the song's lyrics *ky'abeeredde, azinga enkata nga tannalaba kya kwetikka* ("what he is fond of, he rolls a head pad before seeing what to carry") demonstrate how mindful the *kabaka* is of Aboobutiko's needs and his willingness to address such needs before he even learns about them.[1] In return—as was expressed by Ignatio Kawere Ganaayaba, also a Kawuugulu performer and head of a secondary lineage in the Butiko Clan, born in 1919—Aboobutiko willingly serve the *kabaka* without expecting any form of compensation.[2]

To the performer and primary clan lineage head Muhammad Sensonga, born in 1928, "Waggongolo Omutanda" indirectly addresses ineligible performers who attempt to perform with Kawuugulu in order to get close to the *kabaka*. The song warns them against this behavior, ensuring that ineligible performers do not get ahead of themselves.[3] Through such cautioning, "Waggongolo Omutanda" legitimizes Aboobutiko and their ensemble's royal privileges, reminding us of how the griot performers of West Africa assert their historical legitimacy. (Griots have the unique prerogative to face and speak truth to the powerful in ways that others cannot, both in the past and in the present.)[4] This chapter examines Buganda's interactions with the *kabaka* through the intimate relationship he shares with Aboobutiko and their Kawuugulu Ensemble. Focusing on ensemble practices associated with the origins and use of the *Nyamitongo, Nyoolaevvubuka, mpuunyi,* and *Kijoboje* drums as well as the *Kawawa* royal spear, I argue that the clan and ensemble represent other clans before (stand in for them in their special roles vis-à-vis) the *kabaka* while setting themselves apart from those clans. This arrangement allows Kawuugulu, via royal musical performances and storytelling, to manage, structure, model, and legitimize a collaborative relationship between the *kabaka* and his subjects.

Kawuugulu and Royalty

The "Gwa" Rhythm and Dance Movement

Some Kawuugulu performers argue that Aboobutiko interacted with Kintu, the first *kabaka* of Buganda, around the early fourteenth century, through the Kawuugulu musical and dance repertoire. According to an origin story, one of few narratives that associate Kawuugulu with Kintu, the *kabaka* had an elder brother named Lukenge. Lukenge sought the help of a fearless fighter named Bemba, who was allegedly a snake, to overthrow the *kabaka*. Following Kintu's ousting, Aboobutiko embarked on a plan that would enable him to regain governance. Some of the clan leaders helped Kintu flee to the Ssese Islands in Lake Victoria (called Nalubaale in Luganda) in search of advice from sages on how to overthrow Lukenge. Notable among these leaders was a *ggunju*, Butiko Clan head, named Kyebagaba, a probable descendant of the clan's founder Kyebagaba, who was always in Kintu's company. This Kyebagaba served as the primary custodian of the Butiko Clan's drums, *Kawuugulu* and *Kasajja*. He also was the overseer of performances involving the drum pair, of which he was an expert and devout player. Drawing on his performance experience, Kyebagaba initiated the idea of making and tuning a battle drum called *Kyebabona*, which Kintu would use to retake power.[5] For this drum the Butiko Clan created a rhythm known as "Gwa" (Prostrate; see exx. 3.1, 3.2, 3.3, and 3.4).

Luganda	English
Gwa, gwa, gwa.	Prostrate, prostrate, prostrate.

Kyebagaba's expertise and creativity impressed Kintu. As a result, he assigned Kyebagaba responsibilities related to the establishment of exemplary governance in Buganda. The expert artistry that Aboobutiko had displayed in performing on *Kawuugulu* and *Kasajja* further compelled Kintu to appoint them as custodians and principal players of his new battle drum and its rhythm.[6]

Example 3.1. "Gwa" (Prostrate).

Example 3.2. "Gwa," variation 1.

Gwa,   gwa,   gwa,   gwa.

Example 3.3. "Gwa," variation 2.

Gwa,   gwa,   gwa,   gwa,   gwa.   (Gwa,)

Example 3.4. "Gwa," variation 3.

Gwa,   gwa,   gwa, gwa, gwa,   gwa.   (Gwa,)

Just as there are various narratives about Kawuugulu's association with the *kabaka*, there are multiple explanations of the history and use of the "Gwa" drumbeat. According to one story, Aboobutiko were playing the beat on *Kawuugulu* and *Kasajja* before the invention of the *Kyebabona* drum. Kintu brought the drum from the Kingdom of Bunyoro, where he came from and where it was known as *Kumbagara*. Following his arrival in Buganda, the drum's name changed to *Kyebabona* and its players learned the "Gwa" drumbeat from *Kawuugulu* and *Kasajja* drummers. The players of the two drums then taught the beat to some drummers of the Mujaguzo Drums of Kinship. Before long, Mujaguzo drummers were playing "Gwa," using the rhythm to instruct Kintu's subjects to pay him respect through prostrating, particularly whenever they had a royal audience.[7]

According to some sources, however, the Mujaguzo Drums of Kinship came into existence after the reign of Kintu. Moreover, a different story associates "Gwa" with a royal drum called *Mulyabyaki* (literally, "Why do you eat them?").[8] In A. J. Lush's 1935 article "Kiganda Drums" he points out that an unidentified *kabaka* gave *Mulyabyaki* "to the chief of an expedition."[9] Yet another story indicates that during the reign of Kintu's successor, Ssekabaka Cwa I (r. ca. early fourteenth century), some Baganda transformed "Gwa" to "Cwa" to praise Cwa I and to signify his presence.[10]

These stories complementarily highlight music's effect on royal power. The first account parallels similar origin stories about Kintu's interactions with other Kiganda clans. According to Yesoni Nsereko, a Kkobe (Air Potato) Clan member born in 1928, Kintu was a contemporary of the first head of the Kkobe Clan, Nsereko Kalamazi. The two men fought together in various battles. In one of the battles, Bemba (the fighter who was alleged to be a snake) helped Kintu's brother Lukenge to oust the leader. When Kintu was dethroned, he left Buganda with Kalamazi. Because of Kalamazi's help, Kintu was able to recapture power from Bemba. Owing to Kalamazi's shrewdness and fighting skills, Kintu assigned him the responsibility of traveling to the Ssese Islands to locate sages who could help resolve Buganda's administrative challenges. Whenever Kalamazi returned from his expeditions, Kintu inquired about the way he had addressed the sages in Ssese, particularly in their own dialect. In his response, Kalamazi often said *namuyama* ("I welcomed him/her"). However, Kintu often heard the word as *Namwama*, which has no clear meaning in the Luganda language. In time, the misunderstood word was adopted and integrated into the Kkobe Clan's vocabulary. Kintu later chose the term as the official title of the clan head.[11] Like the Butiko Clan head title, *ggunju*, *namwama* is a historical marker of Kintu's interactions with clans.

The *Nyamitongo* Royal Drums

The intimate relationship between Kawuugulu and the *kabaka* is evident in a body of stories about the construction and use of the *Nyamitongo* royal drums. One story, told by Kabenge Gombe, suggests that the clan made these drums for Ssekabaka Mulondo (r. ca. 1524–54), who became heir to the throne as an infant following the unexpected death of his father, Ssekabaka Nakibinge (r. ca. 1494–1524). When Katikkiro (Prime Minister) Kalumba Walusimbi, a primary member of the Ffumbe (Civet Cat) Clan and one of Mulondo's regents, observed that the infant Mulondo appeared miserable during council meetings and public appearances, he was concerned. He advised Mulondo's maternal relatives (Aboobutiko) to devise means of entertaining him. In response to this proposal, the Butiko Clan sought advice from a popular and powerful sage named Nende, who recommended making and tuning a pair of small drums. Aboobutiko would play the drums while dancing to cheer the young Mulondo. Following Nende's guidance, Aboobutiko felled a tree, extracted two blocks from it, and made drum shells or cavities. On behalf of the Buganda government, Katikkiro Walusimbi gave Aboobutiko cows to provide hides to make the drum heads and necessary cords for lacing them. The government also provided goats from which the clan made the original fur belts (*bikuzzi*) that would be worn while dancing to the royal drums. Aboobutiko named the new drums *Nyamitongo* ("Born after Father's Demise"), after the gloom and bewilderment that surrounded Nakibinge's death and Mulondo's enthronement. The drum name combined the words *ny* ("mother of") and *amatongo* ("desolation following calamity").[12] Both terms had roots in the Runyoro language spoken in the Kingdom of Bunyoro that was allegedly prevalent at the time of *Nyamitongo*'s inception.[13]

In a fashion similar to the *Kawuugulu* and *Kasajja* drums, Aboobutiko paired the *Nyamitongo* drums in honor of the belief that every Muganda has a double. They then identified appropriate wood for making the drum pair's beaters and a forked stake (*enkondo ey'amakabi*) to suspend the drums. Given *Nyamitongo*'s royal status, they would not sit on the ground. This stand partly completed the royal status of the drum pair along with the larger Kawuugulu instrumental set; the two drums became a part of the collective when Aboobutiko merged them with *Kawuugulu* and *Kasajja* during the later period of Mulondo's reign. The merger conferred royal status on *Kawuugulu* and *Kasajja* while the drum pair maintained its clan and common statuses. Similarly, the union expanded Kawuugulu's original performance contexts, and elevated the status of Aboobutiko, especially later on when they used the ensemble to serve royalty.[14]

Like the narratives presented in chapter 2, the stories that Aboobutiko told me regarding the origins of *Nyamitongo* were multifaceted in their documentation of various themes, including the individual who spearheaded the drum construction, the role of kingship and the Butiko Clan; the contributions of many different clans; the time period when the invention took place; and the ensemble's role in responding to some of the challenges related to Mulondo's infancy. The Kawuugulu performer George William Kalyemenya, born in 1940, recounted that Buganda's *katikkiro* (prime minister) at the time of *Nyamitongo*'s invention was a primary member of the Butiko Clan, not the Ffumbe Clan. The *katikkiro*'s dual status as both Mulondo's clanmate and as a high-profile administrator made it easy for him to guide Aboobutiko in making the drums. He was also a talented artist who drew on his performance experience to spearhead the construction of the royal drums in question, and to choreograph the dances they accompanied.[15]

In addition, the Kawuugulu performer Yekoyaada Kaggwa Kyagaba, born in 1933, described how Mulondo's maternal relatives, Aboobutiko, realized his loneliness and the need to entertain him without prompting from Buganda's *katikkiro*.[16] And according to Muhammad Sensonga, the spirits (*mmandwa*) that clan elders consulted regarding the construction of Mulondo's drums instructed the clan to cut down a tall tree that stood on a hill called Wampaka and use its wood to make five drums: two large twin drums, one tall drum, and two small drums. When the drums were ready, the clan presented them in Mulondo's palace. Clan members then performed on the drums to entertain Mulondo, a practice that continued whenever he was on his new throne.[17] This is one of the stories that suggest Kawuugulu's inception taking place during the reign of Mulondo.

Edward Ng'anda Mujuuli, a Kawuugulu performer born in 1939, was of the view that Aboobutiko created drums for Mulondo to address his bitter mood, not loneliness.[18] In his 1959 book *Abateregga ku Nnamulondo ya Buganda* (Heirs to the Throne of Buganda), Joseph S. Kasirye writes that a *ggunju* called Najjantyo was the initiator of the plan to invent the drums and their accompanying dances.[19] However, the Kawuugulu performer George Lutwama, born in 1929, suggested that the *ggunju* who led the invention was Luboyera.[20] Ignatio Kawere Ganaayaba pointed out that Mulondo's new royal drums helped cheer him, allowing his caretakers to raise him through childhood, and helping compensate for his father's absence.[21]

Some Aboobutiko narrated stories that partly attribute the creation of *Nyamitongo* and the drum pair's related accessories to the royal stool that the clan constructed for the infant Mulondo. The stool later became Buganda's official throne, *Nnamulondo*. Najjuka Nabagereka, a Kawuugulu dancer born in 1944, suggested that Mulondo's short stature generally prevented people from seeing him easily from a distance, just as it prevented him from seeing them. As a result, Mulondo's maternal relatives made a stool (*ntebe*) to place him on. However, Mulondo appeared lonely on the stool. As a result, Aboobutiko established drums that they used to amuse the prince whenever they placed him on the stool.[22] John Roscoe, in his 1911 book *The Baganda*, writes that Mulondo's subjects could not see him when sitting on the usual rug,[23] yet the historian Kasirye writes that the clan named the stool after the king's mother, the *namasole*, Nnamulondo, who had been carrying Mulondo on her lap in the Buganda parliament, the *Lukiiko*.[24] According to Ganaayaba, *Nyamitongo*'s sounds and their associated dances prevented Mulondo from crying by keeping him lively until he was old enough to walk and stand on his own.[25] Pius Sempa Kawere, a Kawuugulu performer born in 1929, stressed that it was important for Mulondo to smile, a necessity Lutwama highlighted when he indicated that Mulondo's initial smile at the performers signaled his official opening of *Lukiiko*, since he was too young to talk.[26]

But the Kawuugulu performer Fredrick Kaggwa Semugooma, born in 1951, noted that after making the stool, Mulondo's maternal relatives positioned it in the very spot where his mother had previously held him during official meetings, and they continued to entertain him in that space.[27] M. B. Nsimbi, a respected scholar of Kiganda literature and culture and the Luganda language, writes in his 1956 book *Amannya Amaganda n'Ennono Zaago* (Kiganda Names and Their Origins) that the stool later became the official *Nnamulondo* kingship throne, which the prince who became *kabaka* would climb up and sit on, before the head of the Nkima (Monkey) Clan, the *mugema*, tied bark cloth over his shoulder as part of the *kabaka*'s coronation rites.[28]

According to another set of stories, the use of the royal drums inspired the construction of the royal stool, not the other way around. Muhammad

Sensonga stated that a Butiko clansman named Katimbo led the clan in constructing the stool. But Mulondo appeared passive while sitting on it, raising new concerns as to how well Buganda would fare under a dull leader. These concerns in turn inspired the making of drums, which eventually prompted Mulondo to learn how to speak, for when he grew older he occasionally touched the drums and imitated their sounds.[29] But another respected historian of Kiganda culture, Sir Apolo Kagwa, writes in *Ekitabo Kye Bika bya Baganda* (A Book about the Clans of the Baganda), published in 1949, that a man called Sekagya collaborated with the *ggunju* at the time to carve the stool.[30] Still, George William Kalyemenya identified a Butiko Clan member and *katikkiro* called Mulondo as the overseer of the stool's construction.[31] However, Fredrick Kaggwa Semugooma credited a *ggunju* called Najjantyo (also mentioned earlier).[32] According to the Kawuugulu dancer Costa Nakyagaba, born in 1971, when Mulondo's maternal relatives made the drums in question, he was too short to see performers on these drums. He compelled his caretakers to create a stool that could raise him high enough to see the drums.[33] However, the Butiko Clan member Anthony Mugagga Muwagga thought that elevating Mulondo also highlighted his supremacy. In addition, the elevation addressed Mulondo's caretakers' concerns about the possibility of his infancy and short stature prohibiting his subjects from giving him the respect owed to a leader.[34]

In contrast, a few stories describe the creation of the *Nyamitongo* royal drums and that of the *Nnamulondo* royal throne, or stool, as independent events. In one story Gombe stated that Aboobutiko made the stool for Mulondo only when he was full grown. Following the invention of the stool, Mulondo's mother continued to attend *Lukiiko*, where she knelt beside the stool that later took her name, Nnamulondo.[35] Sir Apolo Kagwa, in *Ekitabo kya basekabaka be Buganda, na be Bunyoro, na be Koki, na be Toro, na be Nkole* (A Book about the Kings of Buganda, Bunyoro, Koki, Toro, and Nkore), published in 1971, writes that the kind of entertainment Mulondo's maternal relatives created for him immediately after carving his stool never involved royal drums. According to Kagwa, the drums came much later, when Mulondo was a man, and Aboobutiko carved the stool after performing the final funeral rites of his father. Aboobutiko then selected young boys capable of dancing, and guided them in entertaining Mulondo whenever he appeared before his subjects on the stool. When Mulondo was a grown man, his mother also died. Heartbroken, he barely left his palace. When the *ggunju* realized that Mulondo was overcome with sorrow, he made him the royal drums and brought them into the palace, or *lubiri*, where Aboobutiko performed on them, dancing the way they had when he was still a boy. When Mulondo heard the drums, he came out to the palace to see them. One of his maternal uncles asked him to look at his sisters and select a potential heiress, or *musika*, to his mother. Mulondo selected the sister who bore a striking resemblance to his late mother to serve as her heiress. Following this occasion, the drums Aboobutiko had made to console Mulondo became the property of the Butiko Clan.[36]

Multiple origin stories and their variations bring out different aspects of dance practices associated with Mulondo's drums. As one of the stories presented earlier indicates, the need to entertain him at official functions led Kawuugulu dancers to create dances that would accompany his new drums. Accordingly, Nende, the sage mentioned in the opening story, advised Aboobutiko to seek permission from the head of the Ngeye (Colobus Monkey) Clan, the *kasujja*, to hunt colobuses. Hides of these animals served as additional fur belts (*bikuzzi*) for dancers. The *kasujja* willingly granted the permission because his daughter, Nakasujja, had married a *ggunju* named Luboyera. The headquarters of the Ngeye and Butiko Clans were located next to each other, in Busujja and Bukalango. Nende further recommended that the dancers wear pellet bells (*ndege*) on their ankles whenever they danced to Mulondo's new royal drums. The sounds of the bells would also amuse the infant and help to quiet him when he was crying.[37] Contrary to this narrative, however, Ganaayaba noted that the Ngeye Clan provided readymade fur belts for dancing.[38]

Other accounts elaborate on the dances associated with Mulondo's drums. According to Semugooma, they included a dance that featured movements in which the performers jumped high around Mulondo's drums and his royal stool playfully.[39] Muwagga's account indicated that the performers also danced backward.[40] Elaborating on the dance in question, Ganaayaba stated that when Mulondo's caretakers realized that it made him smile and sometimes even leap on his mother's lap, they used it to open official meetings when he was presiding. His initial smiles at the performers came to serve as the official openers of the meetings, and this practice lasted until he was old enough to talk. After smiling, the *katikkiro* would instruct Mulondo's maternal relatives to take him away from the meetings before they continued.[41]

In another story, Gombe stated that during Mulondo's reign, Okubina became the official and universal descriptor of Kawuugulu dancing style; it involved jumping and lifting or raising legs very high. The term had originally referred to the concluding dance of the ensemble's performances. However, Okubina came to encompass all Kawuugulu dances after its style became more popular than those of all of the other styles. Similarly, the label's derivative term, Ababinyi ("Jumpers" or "Raisers") became the official label for Kawuugulu dancers.[42] Following this transformation, another dance, known as "Okugaba," which had originated during the reign of Ssekabaka Kimera, replaced Okubina as the new closing dance of Kawuugulu performances.[43]

Some accounts stress that Amaggunju—"dances associated with the *ggunju*"—a popular alternate name for all Kawuugulu dances, also came into existence during Mulondo's reign. According to Kalyemenya, the clan labeled Kawuugulu dances Amaggunju to acknowledge the strong hand of the *ggunju* in the affairs of Mulondo. These affairs included taking charge of raising him and ensuring the smooth running of his administration.[44] The historians Kasirye, Nsimbi, and Lush suggest that the term Amaggunju was derived from Bannaggunju, the term for official performers of Amaggunju. The term, as already mentioned, can be translated as "the dances associated with the *ggunju*."[45] Kasirye identifies the *ggunju* in question as Najjantyo, suggesting that he established and directed Kawuugulu performances by selecting child dancers for the infant Mulondo, who occasionally performed with the children.[46] However, Gombe believed that the term Amaggunju originated from mishearing the songs "Aga Ggunju" (The Dance of the *Ggunju*), "Eza Ggunju" (The Ankle Bells of the *Ggunju*), and "Aba Ggunju" (The Performers of the *Ggunju*). As discussed in chapter 2, the songs were associated with the *Kawuugulu* and *Kasajja* drums and came into existence during the reign of Ssekabaka Kimera to signal the role of the *ggunju* in developing and leading Kawuugulu performances. However, the songs became more established during Mulondo's era, when Kawuugulu performers merged his new royal drums with *Kawuugulu* and *Kasajja*.[47]

The foregoing accounts highlight how a familial relation became a political one, and how the two were consubstantial. The dawn of Kawuugulu's protective and entertainment responsibilities depended on an alliance, spearheaded by Aboobutiko, of different entities, including the Buganda government, various clans and their leaders, sages, invisible powers, and others. These entities shaped the complex, interwoven, counterbalanced voices and political relationships between the Butiko Clan and Mulondo. The relationships are evident in the way Aboobutiko used the *Nyamitongo* drums to nurture Mulondo when he was still young. One of the meanings of the drum name, "Born after father's demise," reflects how the clan facilitated his growth and helped engender his positive appearance before his people. With the help of the drums, the clan cheered his mood, allowing him to make a good impression on his subjects. Aboobutiko helped steer Mulondo in morally and socially righteous directions, enabling him to be an effective and favorable ruler. By assuming a caretaker role for the young, half-orphaned ruler, the clan helped fill the void created by his father's absence, reminding Buganda of Aboobutiko's proprietary relationship to the royal throne. The clan and Mulondo each moved as adroitly as a dancer in maintaining his royal prerogatives through widespread clan support. Similar to some of the ways the griot performers of West Africa have historically emphasized their vital role in the moral shaping of political rule,[48] Aboobutiko and their politics influenced Mulondo's rule. Mulondo depended as much on clan legitimization as the clan depended on him for his favor. These interactions mirror relationships between all clans and the *kabaka* in Buganda.

The various accounts also show the power that Mulondo's subjects accorded him through placing him on the royal stool, highlighting the Baganda's respect for their *kabaka*. Yet the intimate relationship between him and the drums Aboobutiko created for him stressed the instruments' influence on royal power. These dynamics highlight a dually mimetic relationship between the drums and Mulondo, both in imitation of each other. After all, the drums were his, and he was theirs. The instruments served as company to Mulondo, kin in some sense, like faithful comrades to prevent him from being alone. And by allowing for his elevation, which enabled him to see his subjects and for him to be seen, the drums had an effect on mutuality, reciprocity, mimesis, mirroring, and meeting.

Whether it was the royal drums that inspired the creation of the royal stool or the other way round, both motifs are historically valid, since the throne enhanced Mulondo's relationship to both the ensemble and his subjects, and since the drums had to come into being because there was a *kabaka* on the throne. The two motifs seemed to have a chicken-and-egg relationship, demonstrating how the drums situated everyone in a particular place in the hierarchy. Mulondo was to the ensemble as the throne was to the Butiko Clan as the kingship was to all clans. The clan's ensemble was present at all royal meetings. Just as Mulondo encompassed the kingdom, so the Butiko Clan stood in for all other clans, encompassing them in turn. The performative relationship between Mulondo and the ensemble amounted to the constitution of Kiganda sociopolitical life. The relationship has elevated the status of Aboobutiko since Mulondo's reign as one set apart from all others because it represented them, garnering their respect while maintaining royal favor.

The story about performances on *Nyamitongo* consoling Mulondo when he lost his mother reflects the secondary translation of the name of the drum pair: "A Parent Dying Right after His or Her Child's Birth." This translation illustrates how the drums helped the adult Mulondo and how they reflected and confirmed his maturity. Just as, in one of the other stories, they teach him to speak as a boy, here they bring him back to life as an adult. They serve as his double, with the ability to appease his soul. Like many of the stories presented, this story also highlights the importance of the Kiganda analogic kinship practices discussed in the introduction. Mulondo's drums were analogous to him. Their joy made him joyful, and life went on. His sister was like his mother; she took her place, and Mulondo returned to his throne. The kingdom's fate was again secure. Over all, Kawuugulu had a kind of power over Mulondo, a means of guiding him when he was young, that shifted as he grew older and became their patron. In spite of their variations, the accounts presented here reflect an intricately counterweighted balance of powers.

The *Kawawa* Royal Spear

Kawuugulu stories also indicate that during the reign of Mulondo, ensemble members incorporated a royal spear called *Kawawa* into Kawuugulu. Similar to stories about the *Nyamitongo* royal drums and *Nnamulondo* throne, there are many versions of the tale about *Kawawa*'s integration into the ensemble. For example, Nsimbi presents the following account: Mulondo's father, Nakibinge, originally got the spear as a gift from a blacksmith called Buyondo, whom he met on Zinga Island. After obtaining *Kawawa*, Nakibinge left for a town called Bumbu. War broke out there shortly after his arrival, and he entered into the fighting. As Nakibinge tried to flee fighters from the Kingdom of Bunyoro, who were chasing him, he fell with his spear in a trap that unidentified hunters had set to catch buffalo (*mbogo*), and he died there. Many looked for his body in vain. After determining that Nakibinge had vanished, the searchers appointed his son, Omulangira (Prince) Mulondo to succeed him.[49]

Nsimbi's account continues: In the latter part of Mulondo's reign, a hunter who was tracking game in the area where Nakibinge had vanished stumbled upon the spear in a pit, along with human bones. After retrieving the spear, the hunter carried it with him everywhere he went. One day he attended a Kawuugulu performance, and it captivated him. During the performance, some dancers recognized the spear he was holding as Nakibinge's. They immediately seized the hunter and took him to the office of the prime minister, the *katikkiro*, where he was detained and charged with the killing of Nakibinge. On the day of his trial, he explained how he had salvaged the spear from a pit. He added that he had seen human bones there.

The *katikkiro* appointed a committee of judges (*balamuzi*) to go and inspect the pit in the prisoner's company. There they found the human bones, which they retrieved and transported to the *katikkiro*'s office. Some of the people who had known Nakibinge well concluded that the bones were his, because of a gap between his teeth that also had a stain, both of which matched the features of the skull they had examined. But some people still had doubts about the bones and spear being Nakibinge's. Accordingly, the *katikkiro* summoned Buyondo—the blacksmith who had given *Kawawa* to Nakibinge—to testify about the spear. Prior to his arrival, the judges marked the shaft of the spear in question with a tiny spot for identification. The spot was too tiny for anyone to notice except for them. Then they tied up many spears in bundles, and placed *Kawawa* in one of the bundles. Arranging them in a line, they situated the bundle that contained the spear farthest from where they were standing. When Buyondo appeared before the judges, they asked him to find the spear among all the bundles. He began untying them one by one, carefully examining the spears in each one. Eventually, he identified *Kawawa*, which the judges confirmed by the way they had marked it.

There was much rejoicing at the discovery of Nakibinge's remains. The Buganda government eventually released the imprisoned hunter, and ever since, Baganda have said, *Omulonzi tattibwa*, "The finder is not killed," the Luganda equivalent of "Don't shoot the messenger."[50] When Mulondo, now an older leader, learned about these events, he expressed his gratitude to the key people involved in the discovery of his father's remains in a special way. For example, he appointed Buyondo as the head of the royal blacksmiths, called the *walukagga*, declared Aboobutiko the official performers in Kawuugulu, and instructed them to integrate the spear into the ensemble.[51]

Writing about *Kawawa* in 1949, Kagwa credited Kawuugulu performers for arresting, interrogating, and releasing the spear's discoverer. He further established that the *ggunju*, also the overseer of Kawuugulu and the performance that attracted the hunter with *Kawawa*, received much acclaim for the discovery.[52] Kagwa also wrote that the hunter encountered the Kawuugulu event in question while walking to Busujja on the morning following the day on which he found the spear. The pit from which he retrieved *Kawawa* had Nakibinge's shrunken corpse, not bones, which Mulondo saw before the performers transported it to Kitinda. Here they detached Nakibinge's jawbone before burying the rest of the remains, following which they took it to Kongojje to preserve it as per Kiganda protocol.[53] Writing in 1959, Kasirye stated that Mulondo specifically assigned to the *ggunju* the responsibility of integrating *Kawawa* into Kawuugulu.[54]

Similar to the foregoing accounts, my interlocutors' narratives about *Kawawa* differed in their recollections of a number of details: how Nakibinge died with the spear; where and how performers found the spear; how they first identified the man who discovered it and received him at court; how Mulondo celebrated the discovery; how the discoverer identified the spear; how the court identified Nakibinge's body; and when the spear became part of Kawuugulu. Some interviewees narrated stories that indicated that Mulondo declared *Kawawa*'s new place in the ensemble drums immediately following its rediscovery. Others maintained that he was too young at the time to do so, and made that declaration when he was older. Still others depicted the spear's finder as a herdsman who noticed it while tending cattle. And others indicated that the man was a hunter who spotted it beside an animal trap or that the spear was found in a thicket, in an area from which fire had cleared the vegetation, or in an upright position in a pit.

Many narratives also diverged as to how Kawuugulu performers identified *Kawawa* and spotted the man who possessed it. According to some sources, Kawuugulu performers identified the spear by its wide, shiny, bronze head. In other versions the performers recognized it by its unique shaft. According to the latter, the performers were performing under a full moon, which helped them identify the spear. Accounts also differed on the cause of Nakibinge's death, and the discovery and identification of his remains. Some claimed that he had gone out hunting when he fell into a trap for catching game, and died there; others maintained that he died in battle; Nakibinge's nickname, *omulwanyammuli* (literally, "One who fights with reeds"), which acknowledged his exceptional fighting skills, substantiated the latter theory. Still other accounts stated that Kawuugulu performers identified Nakibinge's corpse after examining his skull and noticing a wide gap between his two front teeth.

These myriad tales about *Kawawa*'s history articulate the multifaceted hierarchy at the core of Kiganda politics: kinship, clanship, and kingship. They show, for instance, how the kingship granted the Butiko Clan the responsibility to entertain, protect, praise, and communicate other matters with the *kabaka*. The different stories reflect the kind of diversity both the *kabaka* and clans must recognize in their sociopolitical relationship, a relationship that is as complex as the polymeters that define the music they perform and enjoy together. This diversity is at the heart of Kawuugulu's legitimization of the monarchy in contemporary times.

The *Nyoolaevvubuka*, *Mpuunyi*, and *Kijoboje* Drums

According to some origin stories, after Mulondo's reign, Kawuugulu performers added other drums to the ensemble instrumental set, including *Nyoolaevvubuka*, which many Aboobutiko compare to drums from the Kingdom of Busoga. This comparison is evidence of historical cultural borrowings and exchanges between Buganda and its neighboring interlacustrine kingdoms. Other stories suggested that Aboobutiko acquired the drum as a royal prize from an unidentified *kabaka* who reigned after Mulondo. The prize was for winning a performance competition in which Kawuugulu participated. The clan assigned to the drum a name that combined the Luganda words *nyoola* ("twist") and *evvubuka* ("the stalwart youth"). The compound name *Nyoolaevvubuka* ("Twist the stalwart youth" or "Wrestle down the stalwart youth"), suited the drum's large size and the competitive nature of its acquisition.[55]

Mpuunyi was another drum added to Kawuugulu in the post-Mulondo era, according to some origin stories. One story has it that the Butiko Clan acquired the drum from an unidentified *kabaka*, who rewarded Aboobutiko for their exemplary service to the monarchy.[56] As noted in chapter 2, *mpuunyi* ("hummer"; "moaner")—unlike the proper names *Kawuugulu*, *Kasajja*, *Nyamitongo*, and *Nyoolaevvubuka*—is a generic name for the drum that regulates performance tempo and dancers' timing in many Kiganda ensembles. The use of the drum name among Aboobutiko's Kawuugulu Ensemble demonstrates how the Butiko Clan represents other clans before the *kabaka*.

The origins of these drums and the meanings that Kawuugulu and Aboobutiko attach to them highlight the close relationship between the Butiko Clan and the *kabaka*. For instance, *Nyoolaevvubuka* symbolizes Aboobutiko's excellence over other clans during, and beyond, the competition just mentioned. The origins of the instrument and that of the *mpuunyi* drum also reflects the importance to Kiganda political life of gifts and reciprocity—a complementary relationship of exchange between two or more parties. Indeed, both marriage and blood brotherhood rely upon the giving of gifts, as does hosting of guests. In fact, reciprocity is the central idiom of Kiganda politics, and this applies to performance, too, where drumming, singing, and dancing are presentations to his highness. *Nyoolaevvubuka* and *mpuunyi* are clear markers of the intertwined nature of Kiganda clanship and kingship.

The Butiko Clan identity drum, *Kijoboje*, may be called *mpuunyi*. The name *Kijoboje* translates as "Mumble the text," another indication that Kawuugulu drums can speak like people. Gombe told of a story of the drum's origins whereby the *ggunju* initially used the drum to interact with Mulondo, a primary member of the Butiko Clan. The *ggunju* sounded one of the clan's official *mibala*—melorhythmic patterns or beats with associated textual phrases—on *Kijoboje* whenever he was on his way to visit Mulondo. The *mubala* (sing.) he performed (see ex. 1.1) went as follows: *Weekirikijje; ggunju ajja* ("Prepare yourself in joyful anticipation; the *ggunju* is coming"). This *mubala* announced the arrival at Mulondo's palace of the *ggunju* and of Aboobutiko who escorted him there. On hearing the performances, the *kabaka* prepared to welcome his maternal relatives.[57]

The performance of this *mubala* not only validated the *ggunju*'s leadership but also signified the special status of Butiko Clan members as Mulondo's maternal relatives and royal performers. It is important to note that each clan in Buganda has at least one official *mubala* that it performs on a special clan identity drum. A clan's *mubala* might remind primary members of that clan to value their shared identity, avoid contact with its totems, praise and honor clan ancestors, protect and acknowledge clan estates (*butaka*), guard clan assets and practices, contribute to the clan's sustenance, praise the *kabaka* and his wife, and watch for intruders.[58] It may also invoke ancestral spirits through mediums, who often guide the spirits to address specific social problems within the clan. In addition, a clan *mubala* summons primary members to participate in official events, invites them to confirm ties between the clan and the *kabaka*, and reminds them to praise clan leaders. Although contemporary performances of the Butiko Clan *mubala* at the beginning of Kawuugulu events primarily exalt the *ggunju*, reaffirm his leadership, and welcome him to preside over these events as we saw in chapter 1, the *mubala*'s origins discussed above suggest that it has historically validated Aboobutiko's intimacy with the *kabaka*. Its uses in Kawuugulu performances further demonstrate how Aboobutiko stand apart from other clans while representing them vis-à-vis the *kabaka*. In this way Kawuugulu events highlight the political importance and nature of the ensemble's practice.

Musical Performance, Storytelling, and Royalty

Kawuugulu performers interact with the *kabaka* through the drum rhythm and dance "Gwa" (Prostrate). Ensemble drummers sound "Gwa" on the *Kawuugulu* and *Kasajja* drums, while dancers accentuate its rhythm using the pellet bells they tie around their ankles. This rhythm and dance also have associated textual phrases. "Gwa" is a common feature of performances that lead or protect the *kabaka*. Such performances often prompt his subjects—audience members—to prostrate themselves. Prostrating by the audience amplifies the *kabaka*'s power and influence. In the company of drums, the performers' bell patterns accentuate the rhythms of the drum pair sounding "Gwa" and vice versa. These performances and effects of "Gwa" demonstrate—through rhythm and sound—how Kawuugulu members realize political ideals as embodied practices. The bodies of these performers physically respond to the ensemble's musical sounds, confirming that Kawuugulu drums and human bodies are a lot alike; the instruments have skins, they have insides and outsides, they speak, and they can be played. But "Gwa" also allows Kawuugulu members to protect the *kabaka* through combating his invisible adversaries. In addition, performances of "Gwa" commemorate the support that the Butiko Clan rendered Kintu to recapture power as *kabaka*. In general, "Gwa" legitimizes Aboobutiko's historical collaboration with the *kabaka*, a relationship that in turn signifies similar relationships across other Kiganda clans, some of which are eligible to perform in Kawuugulu.

Drawing on the themes of the stories presented so far, the musical repertoire of Kawuugulu enables the ensemble to articulate Aboobutiko's ties to royalty. Francis Bbirikkadde, a Kawuugulu dancer and dance trainer born in 1934, suggested that the song "Alifumbirwa Nnamulondo" (Whomsoever Nnamulondo Marries; see ex. 3.5) praises the colobus monkey (*ngeye*) fur belts (*bikuzzi*) that Kawuugulu royal dancers tie around their waists during performance.[59]

Luganda	English
Alifumbirwa Nnamulondo,	Whomsoever Nnamulondo marries,
Maama nnyabo!	Dear mother!
N'akaliba ke alikatunda,	He will sell even his small hide,
Maama nnyabo!	Dear mother!

But Lutwama proposed that the song warns men seeking to marry Aboobutiko or Butiko Clan women, to sell their "small hides." For him, *akaliba*, "small hide," is a metaphor for valuables that the groom-to-be would need in order to pay a dowry and provide for his future wife.[60] Nnamulondo is a Butiko clanswoman's name. Accordingly, the song "Alifumbirwa Nnamulondo," as Kalyemenya pointed out, indirectly suggests that Butiko clanswomen are valuable to the monarchy, through praising the clan for producing a woman from whom Buganda's royal throne took its name.[61] This perspective stresses the throne's value. The word *alifumbirwa* literally means "will be cooked for." Thus,

Example 3.5. "Alifumbirwa Nnamulondo" (Whomsoever Nnamulondo Marries).

"Alifumbirwa Nnamulondo" also highlights the importance of cooking in Kiganda marriages. This layering of meanings, similar to the diversity of origins discussed earlier, affirms how kingship depends on clanship as much as Mulondo did on Aboobutiko and their ensemble.

Similarly, the *Nyamitongo* drumbeat "Nnamulondo" and its multiple variations (see exx. 3.6, 3.7, and 3.8) praise and honor Namasole Nnamulondo, Mulondo's mother, for taking care of him while he was an infant.

Example 3.6. "Nnamulondo."

Luganda	English
Nnamulondo,	Nnamulondo,
ddala ddala!	indeed!

Luganda	English
Nnamulondo abina!	Nnamulondo is dancing!

Example 3.7. "Nnamulondo," variation 1.

Example 3.8. "Nnamulondo," variation 2.

Nna-mu - lo - ndo abi - na. (Nna)-(mu)-(lo) -

The beat also praises the kingship throne—which, again, took its official name from Nnamulondo—and validates its existence.[62] These meanings confirm the close relationship between the Butiko Clan and the *kabaka*.

To many Aboobutiko and Kawuugulu members, the ensemble's obligations to protect and entertain the *kabaka* are extensions of the clan's interactions with Mulondo. According to Herbert Mulasa Bbirikkadde Musiitwa, a Kawuugulu custodian born in 1957, these obligations confirm that Aboobutiko parented the *kabaka*.[63] Similarly, the Kawuugulu performer Diriisa Kasiga, born in 1969, noted that the duties highlight the way clan ancestors guided the infant Mulondo.[64] Sensonga told me that the responsibilities in question underscore Aboobutiko's kinship with Mulondo, validating their status as Buganda's "grandparents" (*bajjajja*). This status obliges the clan to protect the *kabaka*, so that the kingdom can successfully continue.[65] In the same vein, the Kawuugulu performer and head of a tertiary lineage head (*owoolunyiriri*) in the Butiko Clan, Bulasio Katimbo, born in 1958, indicated that Kawuugulu's musical protection of the *kabaka* generally validates Aboobutiko's special connection to Kiganda royalty, particularly to Abateregga, the lineage of the reigning *bakabaka*, kings.[66] Yet Kalyemenya noted that the duty commemorates the marriage union between Mulondo's parents, one of whom was a primary member of Butiko Clan.[67] Indeed, when Kawuugulu members perform in the presence of the *kabaka*, they affirm Aboobutiko's historical responsibility of entertaining and protecting Buganda's *bakabaka*.

Since Mulondo's times Kawuugulu performers have addressed each other as Ababinyi, a term that literally means "Raisers" or "Jumpers." Similarly, the performers have referred to their dancing style as Okubina (literally, "dancing while jumping and lifting or raising legs very high"). According to Yisaaya Ng'anda, the use of these terms in contemporary times also expresses Aboobutiko's historical practice of entertaining Mulondo and subsequent *bakabaka*.[68] For Lutwama also, the jumping or kicking that Kawuugulu dancers do is very similar to that of Mulondo's performers.[69] As the practices of dances and vocabulary from Mulondo's time characterizing Kawuugulu dance practice today demonstrate, the ensemble embodies a long history of collaboration between the *kabaka* and Aboobutiko. The use of the terms Ababinyi and Okubina are markers of Mulondo's influence on

Kawuugulu dance. Contemporary ensemble performers and Aboobutiko also refer to Kawuugulu dances as Amaggunju, "dances associated with the *ggunju*," a practice some trace back to Mulondo's reign. The continued use of this name speaks to present configurations of power, just as it speaks to the past. In particular, the use of the term shows how Butiko Clan leadership and Kawuugulu dance performance are generally inseparable. Certainly, contemporary Kawuugulu dance practices highlight the intimate relationship between the clan and the *kabaka*.

Like Mulondo's performers, contemporary Kawuugulu dancers wear pellet bells around their ankles. According to Jamaada Maviirinkata, a Kawuugulu lead dancer and dance trainer born in 1947, these bells help access the supernatural power that sustains Kawuugulu's political relevance. Their sounds summon the ancestral spirits that possess the dancers, empowering them to keep the *kabaka* safe. These spirits include Nende, Kawuula, Nkyeru, and Lukwata. Some of these names are those of ancestors associated with the Butiko Clan.[70] Because ankle bells help summon ancestral spirits in other Kiganda rituals that invoke ancestral spirits to possess invokers (*kusamira*), their use in Kawuugulu royal performances demonstrates how the Butiko Clan and its ensemble constitute sociopolitical practices common across other clans in the Kingdom of Buganda.

Another contemporary practice that validates the intimacy between the Aboobutiko and royalty via Kawuugulu is placing the *Nyamitongo* drums associated with Mulondo at the front of the ensemble's instrument setup, and positioning them higher than other drums of the Kawuugulu drum set. This practice highlights *Nyamitongo*'s royal status, reminding performers of Kawuugulu's agency and the role of historical narratives in shaping contemporary practice. Similarly, Kawuugulu performers place the *Kawawa* royal spear (associated with Mulondo's father, Nakibinge) among ensemble drums to mark their royal identity. The spear being a tool of authority and protection in Buganda—traditionally most household heads owned spears—*Kawawa*'s presence in Kawuugulu confirms Aboobutiko's defense obligations to the *kabaka*. In addition, ensemble members generally associate the tunics (*kkanzu*) they wear with Kiganda royalty, in part because the robes recall a period in the history of Buganda when the *kabaka* adopted them. According to many ensemble members, performing in these tunics signifies and accentuates their closeness to the *kabaka*. Mujuuli pointed out that Kawuugulu performers may dress in other outfits when performing at Butiko Clan occasions such as final funeral rites, but they must dress in tunics when performing at functions attended by the *kabaka*, given their royal nature.[71] Because members of other clans wear tunics in royal contexts, the use of the fabrics in Kawuugulu royal events shows how the Butiko Clan stands in for all other clans in its performances vis-à-vis the *kabaka*.

Kawuugulu's Influence on Royal Power and Clan Authority

This chapter presents abundant evidence that the Butiko Clan has historically had an intimate relationship with the *kabaka* via Kawuugulu. This relationship makes Aboobutiko and their ensemble important institutions in Buganda. Through musical performance and storytelling, the ensemble validates its influence on royal power, just as it validates the dependence of clan authority on that power. Through Aboobutiko's obligation to protect and entertain the *kabaka* via Kawuugulu musical events, the ensemble articulates and constitutes clanship and kingship, both of which are mediated by kinship. The inextricable relationship of these domains is archived in the stories about the creation and acquisition of the drums discussed in this chapter. Some stories indicated that Aboobutiko received two drums from royalty as forms of recognition for the Butiko Clan's excellence over other clans (competition and service). Each of the drums discussed, and many other items that ensemble performers include in its musical events, reflects Kawuugulu's encompassing symbolic nature—of clans, historic periods, and the emblematic kingship in the ensemble's caretaker relationship to royalty (particularly Mulondo). The diversity of ensemble items, like the variety of stories about them, reinforces the constitution of the kingdom as a balance of diverse, sometimes conflicting, forces that can nonetheless find harmony. Kinship, clanship, and kingship define Aboobutiko and Kawuugulu's identity within Buganda and the many clans this group and its ensemble represent. By performing on musical instruments that speak to and for the *kabaka*, for example, Aboobutiko mark their special, intimate status with him and within the kingdom. Certainly, the clan speaks for all clans through its ensemble, and also to all clans. And it stands in for them all in its performative duties, as its drumbeats, songs, dances, and stories perform the relational nature of Kiganda politics.

Chapter Four

Kawuugulu and Inter-Clan Politics

Primary members of the Butiko Clan, Aboobutiko, have kin ties to other clans. These connections revolve around various forms of blood ties, which allow certain secondary members of the Butiko Clan to perform with Kawuugulu. Goreti Nalugunju, a Kawuugulu performer and primary member of the clan born in 1982, stressed that the ensemble's drums can distinguish a performer with clan blood from a person without affiliation.[1] Another primary member of the clan and Kawuugulu performer, Diriisa Kasiga, born in 1969, recounted an event where an ineligible performer tried to dance to the ensemble's drum set during a performance in the *kabaka*'s palace in Banda during the late 2000s. According to Kasiga, the performer stiffened after ignoring the counsel of eligible performers who had asked him to stop dancing. Fortunately, he lived despite this near-death experience.[2]

Annet Najjuka, a primary clan member and Kawuugulu performer born in 1946, stated that another ineligible performer dared dance with the ensemble during the same event. His intention was to verify that Kawuugulu drums could actually incapacitate individuals without Butiko Clan blood. The victim instantly began to suffer from an abdominal disorder that caused him to drop to the ground. Ensemble members removed him from the performance area before his condition became fatal.[3] I recorded numerous such accounts from performers who had witnessed Kawuugulu drums incapacitate non-ensemble members who tried either to walk through the instruments or to touch them during the early twentieth-century.

In this chapter I focus on how Kawuugulu draws on musical performance and storytelling to model and structure connections between Aboobutiko and primary members of other clans. As the events and practices recounted in the foregoing narratives show, the ensemble is able to "distinguish," "exclude," and "embrace" members of Kiganda society, thus acting as a system of inter-clan politics.[4]

Butiko and Ngeye Clan Relations

Abengeye, primary members of the Ngeye (Colobus Monkey) Clan, are eligible performers in Kawuugulu because of their connections to Aboobutiko through historical blood brotherhood (*mukago*) and marriage alliances (*bufumbo*). Both groups believe that these connections established kinship that qualifies Abengeye to perform in the ensemble. Najjuka Nabagereka told me that this kinship was so strong that at one point many members considered not intermarrying between the Butiko and Ngeye Clans in fear of committing incest.[5] Some origin stories suggest that the historical *mukago* between the two clans predated and encouraged marriage alliances that impacted Kawuugulu performances. According to one story, before the reign of Ssekabaka Kayima (r. ca. 1464–94), a Ngeye clanswoman named Nakasujja who was the daughter of an unidentified Ngeye Clan head (*kasujja*), married a Butiko Clan head (*ggunju*) named Luboyera. The couple had a daughter named Nnaabagereka Nakayima, who gave birth to Kayima. Because of Aboobutiko's relationship with the *kabaka*, they acquired the honorable title *ssaabaganzi* ("father of all beloved").[6] They also became the official maternal uncles (*bakkojja*) of the reigning monarchy. During Kayima's reign, a severe famine struck Buganda, leading to a widespread consumption of banana rhizomes (*nkolo*).[7] Eating these rhizomes compelled some Baganda to nickname the famine *Kiryankolo* ("Period of surviving on rhizomes"). Many Aboobutiko survived without consuming them, however, because their clanmate Kayima welcomed them in his palace, where there was plenty of edible food.

But many primary members of other clans, who did not have the same privilege, died from starvation. When the famine ended, Aboobutiko composed and performed the songs "Ensawo Zaffe Bbiri" (Our Two Amniotic Sacs; ex. 4.1) and "Ensuku Zaffe Bbiri" (Our Two Plantations; ex. 4.2) to commemorate some of their experiences.

Luganda	English
Ensawo zaffe bbiri,	Our two amniotic sacs,
ezaatuwonya enkolo;	which saved us from rhizomes;
eya ggunju n'eya kasujja.	of the *ggunju* and of the *kasujja*.

Example 4.1. "Ensawo Zaffe Bbiri" (Our Two Amniotic Sacs).

E - nsa-wo za - ffe bbi -ri, e - zaa - tu - wo-nya e-nko-lo;
e - ya ggu - nju n'e - ya ka - su - jja.

Luganda	English
Ensuku zaffe bbiri,	Our two plantations,
ezaatuwonya enkolo;	which saved us from rhizomes;*
olwa ggunju n'olwa kasujja.	of the *ggunju* and of the *kasujja.***

*Performers may replace the phrase *ezaatuwonya enkolo* with *ze zaatuwonya enkolo* ("are the ones which saved us from rhizomes"), *ze zaatuwonya enjala* ("are the ones which saved us from hunger"), or *mwe twalyanga emmere* ("in which we used to eat food"). The texts generally share the same rhythmic pattern.

**Performers may also replace the phrase *olwa ggunju n'olwa kasujja* with *ggunju ne kasujja* ("the *ggunju* and the *kasujja*") or *Munnaggunju abina* ("the *ggunju*'s performer is dancing") or *ka nneekirikijje ondabe* ("let me flaunt myself in joyful anticipation of your attention").

Example 4.2. "Ensuku Zaffe Bbiri" (Our Two Plantations).

These songs commemorated how such marriage alliances, and the blood brotherhood that predated them, enabled a large population of the Butiko Clan to survive the famine.[8]

There are various narratives about the origins and meanings of "Ensawo Zaffe Bbiri" and "Ensuku Zaffe Bbiri." George William Kalyemenya, a Kawuugulu performer born in 1940, noted that the songs celebrated a later marriage between an unidentified *ggunju* and a Ngeye clanswoman. The couple had a daughter called Nnaabagereka Nnamulondo, whom Ssekabaka Nakibinge (r. ca. 1494–1524) married. They begat Ssekabaka Mulondo, a primary member of the Butiko Clan.[9] These varied accounts strengthen the idea that Aboobutiko and Abengeye have historically shared ties via blood brotherhood and marriage alliances. However, according to Mike Kasirye, a Kawuugulu performer who was born in 1943, the groups' historical brotherhood enabled them to survive the *Kiryankolo* famine because they shared food from each other's plantations. He added that during the famine, the plantations eventually ran out of edible bananas. The shortage compelled the survivors to eat rhizomes as food, which they collected from their plantations. After the famine the survivors celebrated these events through the songs about the famine.[10]

Different interviewees made different statements about the meaning of "Ensawo Zaffe Bbiri" and "Ensuku Zaffe Bbiri." According to Gombe, the term *ensawo*, "amniotic sacs," in the first song acknowledges the wombs of Nakasujja and Nakayima, both of whom made the marriage alliances explained earlier possible. That is, the sacs allowed for the conception of Omulangira (Prince) Kayima, a Butiko clansman who later became *kabaka*.[11] Gombe added that the term *ensuku*, "the plantations," in the second song also refers to the Butiko and Ngeye Clans and the elevated statuses they acquired following the marriage alliances in question.[12] Kalyemenya provided a somewhat different explanation, stating that *ensuku* is a metaphor for the genitals of the *ggunju* and Ngeye Clan woman who produced Nnaabagereka Nnamulondo, wife of Ssekabaka Nakibinge and mother of Ssekabaka Mulondo (discussed in chapter 3). The metaphor highlights the role reproduction played in cementing the alleged brotherhood between the two clans in question.[13] To Bulasio Katimbo, a Kawuugulu dancer and head of a tertiary lineage (*owoolunyiriri*) in the Butiko Clan, born in 1958, the word *ensuku* acknowledges the importance of the heads of the two clans, highlighting their high status, leadership roles, and historical closeness.[14] Still, the Kawuugulu performer Goreti Nalugunju, born in 1982, argued that the term *ensuku* refers to different historic places associated with just the Butiko Clan. She stated that the clan ancestors and the brothers Semagonge and Kajugujwe separated, after which one of them traveled to Koome and the other followed a stream that led him to Buziranjovu. These two places are "the plantations" that the song refers to.[15]

Numerous Kawuugulu performers also mentioned that *ensuku* symbolized the historical estates or permanent places of residence (*butaka*) of Aboobutiko and Abengeye. According to Muhammad Sensonga, a Kawuugulu dancer and head of a primary lineage head (*owessiga*) in the Butiko Clan born in 1928, the proximity of the two clans' estates and the plantations on which they were situated enabled them to share food during the famine.[16] The Kawuugulu performer Charles Lutaaya Muwaga, born in 1924, explained that the estates were on two neighboring hills with a valley between them. The estate of Abengeye was on a hill in a village called Busujja, and that of Aboobutiko was on a hill in a village called Bukalango. Because the estates were adjacent, children from the two groups played together. These interactions bonded the children, leading their families and descendants to become closer kin who, as mentioned earlier, at one point almost considered intermarriage between the Ngeye and Butiko Clans incestuous. In other words, the interactions made the already existing blood brotherhood between the two clans even stronger.[17]

But Hannington Joshua Kizza Mugwanya, a Kawuugulu performer born in 1956, said that the forefathers of Aboobutiko and Abengeye, whom "Ensuku Zaffe Bbiri" also commemorates, strengthened the kinship between their families through tilling the two neighboring plantations.[18] The forefathers also collaborated as warriors and medicine men, as Sensonga pointed out.[19] Moreover Matia Kawere, also a Kawuugulu dancer and the twenty-fifth *ggunju*, stated that Aboobutiko and Abengeye's forefathers shared a rock on which they ground herbal medicines.[20] Yisaaya Ng'anda a Kawuugulu performer born in 1943, explained that the rock became a point of unity between the two clans.[21]

Multiple Kawuugulu stories stress different points, just as different ensemble rhythms can coexist. The complexly overlapping nature of the ensemble's narratives, therefore, results in alternate interpretations among its members. Despite the conflicting details, the accounts seem to suggest that the blood brotherhood between Aboobutiko and Abengeye was the crucial element that enabled either outcome of the alleged famine. The forms of collaboration that these stories highlight underline the role of residence and proximity in maintaining close kinship in Buganda.

Every Kiganda clan historically possesses one or multiple estates called *butaka* that keep primary members of that clan closer together. Gombe, in his explanation of the term's history, noted that after stabilizing Buganda, Ssekabaka Kintu (r. ca. early fourteenth century) recognized his chiefs and other individuals of stature such as royals by allotting them plots of land (*bibanja*). These individuals used the land for growing food, constructing shelters, rearing animals, and establishing settlements for their grown children, close relatives, and servants. Assigning someone a plot, *kibanja* (sing.), made him a resident owner of a permanent place of abode (*mutuuze*), as well as an eligible appointee to the *kabaka*'s service.[22] A recipient of a *butaka* from the *kabaka* became qualified for the status of *mutaka*. A man who never met this criterion was simply known as *musajja wa kabaka*, a king's subject. When a *mutaka* died, the *kabaka*'s administration recommended a replacement who would take charge of the deceased's *butaka*, title, and administrative responsibilities. In a way, land remained the *kabaka*'s permanent property, and a *mutaka* maintained ownership over it only while he was still alive.[23]

Today the term *mutaka* serves as one of the universal titles of a clan head in Buganda, highlighting the close relationship between residence or land (*ttaka*) and sociopolitical organization. The *kabaka*'s permanent ownership of all land is the basis of his title *ssaabataka*, which may translate as "the father of all *bataka* (pl. of *mutaka*)." The use of these labels also affirms the relevance of residence to administration within Buganda's kinship, clanship, and kingship institutions. Serving as permanent residences for both the living and the dead, clan *butaka* facilitate the coexistence of the visible and invisible worlds as well as the blood brotherhood and other performative kin ties that the occupants share. In Buganda, residence also strengthens relations between members of different clans, particularly when the individuals and groups are neighbors. Thus, the Kiganda proverb *Omuliraano ogutegeeregana gusiinga oluganda* ("Neighborhood that gets along is better than kinship"). These practices emphasize the performative nature of Kiganda kinship. For instance, blood brotherhood, marriage, and neighborliness create kinship through performance and that kinship results in further performance.

Musical Performance, Blood Brotherhood, and Affinity

As already established, Abengeye perform with Kawuugulu because their ancestors engaged in blood brotherhood and marriage alliances with those of Aboobutiko. The songs "Ensawo Zaffe Bbiri" and "Ensuku Zaffe Bbiri" encourage Abengeye to join in the ensemble's performances, thus affirming the kinship they have with Aboobutiko. The Kawuugulu performer and secondary clan lineage head (*owoomutuba*) Ignatio Kawere Ganaayaba, born in 1919, said that when the ensemble starts performing the songs, Abengeye involved in its events become very excited. Those performing with the ensemble may begin jumping high, while non-performers sitting down may rise up to join in the official performers' singing.[24] Ensemble events draw Abengeye and Aboobutiko closer. According to Ganaayaba, Aboobutiko give Abengeye the first priority to perform in Kawuugulu because they are closest to them. They let them touch the ensemble's drumsticks (*minyolo*), to which primary members of other clans never come close.[25] These practices demonstrate how blood brotherhood and Kawuugulu performance practice shape each other. Musical practice serves as a kind of shared substance for those who share other forms of shared substance such as blood. Blood brotherhood shapes Kawuugulu musical performance to the extent that musical performance shapes blood brotherhood relations. In other words, the ensemble's musical practice is political practice to the extent that blood brotherhood shapes political realities.

Some Abengeye have access to Kawuugulu from childhood, as described by Yozefiina Nakitto, a Kawuugulu dancer and born in 1929. When Nakitto, a Ngeye Clan member, was three, she lived with her eldest sister, who was married to the late Pantaleo Dibya. Dibya was a *ggunju*, and the couple's home was located next to the Butiko Clan estate in Bukalango, which was a hotbed of many Kawuugulu rehearsals and performances in the 1930s. Through these performances, Nakitto interacted with knowledgeable and skilled performers from whom she learned about the ensemble. The performers included the renowned dancers and dance trainers Nabasazi and Kakunu, who taught her how to perform the "Waggongolo" dance (named after the "Waggongolo Omutanda" song); an exceptional dancer named Nsambu, from whom she learned how to soar high during the aerial dance called "Okwawula" ("Dividing");[26] and a renowned dancer called Katabulwa, who introduced her to a number of performance eligibility customs.[27] Nakitto's involvement with Kawuugulu demonstrates how the ensemble's dance and the means of learning about it occur as a result and confirmation of blood brotherhood and affinal ties to the Butiko Clan. Like Nakitto's, many Kawuugulu members' performance careers are involved with family and clan matters.

Aboobutiko who perform in contemporary Kawuugulu believe that the ensemble's use of colobus monkey (*ngeye*) fur belts for dancing as well as sheep (*ndiga*) skin ankle bands and cords helps sustain their relationship with the Ngeye and Ndiga Clans. As one of the stories in chapter 3 revealed, Abengeye supplied Aboobutiko with colobus monkey skins to make the dance fur belts that Kawuugulu dancers tied around their waists while entertaining Ssekabaka Mulondo. Consequently, since Mulondo's reign, Abengeye have enjoyed a strengthened relationship with Kawuugulu and have been eligible to participate in the ensemble's performances with Aboobutiko.

Similarly, various stories indicate a history of collaboration between the Butiko and Ndiga Clans during some of the events related to Kawuugulu's development. According to a story recounted by Gombe, before making the *Nyamitongo* drums for Mulondo, the Butiko Clan approached the head of the Ndiga Clan, the *lwomwa*, and sought his permission to slaughter sheep. From their skins the clan would make cords for tying the pellet bells that dancers wore around their ankles while performing on the new drums. Sheep hides also were used to make ankle bands that the performers wore underneath the bells. The Butiko Clan had to request the Ngeye and Ndiga Clans' permission before slaughtering colobus monkey and sheep and using their skins, because the two clans regarded these animals as their primary totems.[28]

Kawere noted that the colobus monkey fur belts that contemporary Kawuugulu performers tie around their waists while dancing primarily serve to draw the Butiko and Ngeye Clans together and to strengthen their historical kin ties—and they also help make ensemble events more visually attractive.[29] This is also true of the sheepskin bands that dancers wrap around their ankles before tying pellet bells onto them. Some Aboobutiko emphasize that these accessories—along with the sheepskin cords that fasten the bells—highlight their close ties to the Ndiga Clan. These bands additionally protect the dancers from soreness that might result from the bells rubbing against their ankles during performance. In the context of Kawuugulu events, sheep and colobus monkey hides are embodied material and a form of shared substance that Aboobutiko wear as totems of their Ngeye and Sheep Clan relatives. Similar to the accessories discussed above, various items in Kawuugulu serve as tools of validating historical kinship between Aboobutiko and Abengeye.

Abengeye's participation in Kawuugulu and the beliefs and practices associated with such participation model and reflect *mukago*, blood brotherhood, dynamics in Buganda. Traditionally, *mukago* has allowed Baganda of different clans and ancestries to establish kinship. In his historical account of this ritual, John Roscoe writes that two men who agree to become relatives meet with witnesses and representatives from their respective clans, normally also including their immediate families. The parties, usually men, sit opposite each other on a bark cloth and divide a coffee bean. Each then slightly cuts his stomach, takes one of the bean halves, rubs it in his blood, and places it in the other man's palm, then both swallow their exchanged halves. Following this alliance, the two men, now brothers and members of each other's clans, pledge allegiance to each other, vowing to help each other and assist members of each other's families when in need.[30]

Historically, breaking a *mukago* rule was a serious offense. According to Margaret Chave Fallers, *mukago* rites were "considered a sacred and binding pledge, [the] breach of which would be followed by sickness and death."[31] In his 1934 study *The Customs of the Baganda*, Sir Apolo Kagwa writes that if a man cheated his partner during (and probably after) a *mukago* ritual, the cheated cursed the cheater, who became ill or died from the curse: "There were some people who cheated while taking the oath. For instance, some would spit out the coffee bean instead of swallowing it. Doing this sort of thing often made a man very sick. Their mouths might swell or become twisted, or they might have some other deformity, plainly advertising their trickery." A man guilty of cheating his partner compensated him by preparing him a meal. During the meal, the cheated brother dipped a small serving of banana, *matooke*, in goat stew (a staple meal) and gave it to the guilty one, telling him that he had completely forgiven him. The cheater admitted his mistake, also dipping a small serving of *matooke* in goat stew and giving it to his partner. He also asked his colleague to pray for him in order to free him from the curses his *mukago* relative had placed on him. In some instances, the guilty man gave a young relative to his partner as a hostage until they settled the matter.[32] A *mukago* relationship was a lifetime commitment.

Mukago rites transformed the social status and identity of many initiates in precolonial and colonial Buganda. Fallers writes that most fathers attempted to have their sons strategically become *mukago* relatives with at least one member of another clan. Later in life, the sons were free to enter into a similar relationship with people of other clans of their choice.[33] Bro. A. Tarcis Nsobya notes that such individuals were mainly captives who surrendered to Baganda people during wars. A captor and captive could easily enter into *mukago* if the two became friends; the latter would become a member of the former's clan. In some cases, captives secretly lured children of their captors or masters to enter into the *mukago* relationship with them. In both of these cases, captives became members of their captors' clans.[34] Kagwa writes that if a domestic servant (different from a captive) of a chief entered into *mukago* with a son of that chief, the status of the servant rose. Kings had the power to execute any of their subjects, but they rarely executed men with whom they had made *mukago* oaths.[35] Because *mukago* allowed social mobility within an otherwise strict hierarchy by allowing non-Baganda people to become members of Kiganda clans, the rite was of crucial importance.

Mukago rites are rare in recent years, in part due to fear of contracting HIV/AIDS from infected blood. But it is still important in the way it highlights the emphasis many Baganda place on blood in the creation of kinship that grants initiates membership into clans to which they have no prior ancestral links, and which promote membership in multiple clans. Nevertheless, *mukago* ties have certain limits, which are evident in various discriminative practices. Peter Kinene, a Lugave (Pangolin) Clan member born in 1969, explained that some clans traditionally initiate children and grandchildren of their *mukago* relations differently from their own. Similarly, when those children and grandchildren die, the clans bury them on the far sides of the clans' burial sites (*bijja*), far from the graves of original clan children and grandchildren.[36] There are varied levels of consanguinity in the Kiganda society.

These relationships are also reflected in Kawuugulu performance. Muwaga told me that when he was still a student in Nsambya, he met a Ngeye clansman. After learning that Muwaga was a primary member of the Butiko Clan, the man treated him like his own son. The man told Muwaga that he was always welcome to stop by his house in Konge, and that whenever he was walking from school he should come over to drink some water before proceeding to his home in Salaama. In turn, Muwaga treated Aboobutiko like family, encouraging them to take part in Kawuugulu performances.[37] Marshall Sahlins writes in his discussion of the idea of "mutuality of being" that true kinship implies that the parties involved play active and intrinsic roles in each other's lives.[38] The ways in which Kawuugulu performers treat *mukago* as kinship speak to the practice of active familial ties.

Bajjwa Performers

Although Butiko clanswomen's children, *bajjwa*, (sing. *mujjwa*) are primary members of other clans, they are eligible performers with Kawuugulu based on their blood ties to the clan through their mothers. Statements such as "they are children of our sisters," "we are their mothers," "they carry our clan blood," or "our clan blood circulates within their domains" are common among Aboobutiko. Umaru Mukasa Kavuma—a *mujjwa* (clanswoman's child), primary member of the Ngo (Leopard) Clan, and Kawuugulu dancer born in 1942—stated that he had performed in Kawuugulu since his childhood. Some of his matrilineal kin took him in at age five after he lost his father. Most of these relatives were members of the Bayegga primary lineage (*ssiga*) of the Butiko Clan, which is traditionally responsible for producing *baggunju*, Butiko Clan heads. Owing to his status as a *mujjwa* in the Butiko Clan, Aboobutiko encouraged him to participate in Kawuugulu performances and to learn from skilled and knowledgeable performers. Kavuma was fortunate to learn from several, including his grandfather Kikwekwe, who was a skilled player of *Kawuugulu* and *Kasajja* as well as a trainer of the drum pair's players; a clan elder named Lunnabe, who was renowned for playing and teaching the *Nyamitongo* drum pair; another clan elder named Kereti, a master player of *Nyamitongo*; and Balinnya, a *ggunju* who played *Kawuugulu* and *Kasajja*. Balinnya's drumming often enticed Kavuma to dance for extended periods, allowing him to refine his performance skills.[39] Kavuma's experiences confirm that Butiko *bajjwa* gain full access to Kawuugulu in spite of their secondary membership in the clan. His experiences mirror my own experiences and the access I had to the ensemble.

The *Bajjwa*'s cultural power is based on the belief that they can neutralize spells among their matrilineal kin, and this underpins their performances in Kawuugulu. Because of this status, Kavuma said, Aboobutiko continually see his participation in the ensemble's performances as a way of defusing unbecoming spirits that trouble them. This position gives him even greater access to many sacred traditions of the ensemble, and allows him to master them better than many primary members of the clan.[40] Mindful of their special position in the Butiko Clan, the clan's *bajjwa* participate in Kawuugulu's events on a regular basis. The Kawuugulu performer Erasmus Kyagaba Binywera, born in 1933, recounted that the clan had a *mujjwa* named Bisaso who was a stunning Kawuugulu dancer; his skills exceeded those of many Aboobutiko.[41] During my fieldwork, Butiko Clan *bajjwa* proved their deep understanding of Kawuugulu by addressing technical issues about the ensemble's history and practice in ways that some Aboobutiko could not.

Just as Kawuugulu models and reflects *mukago* dynamics in Buganda, the ensemble's practices highlight the social power of *bajjwa* within the kingdom. I witnessed this power firsthand during an anonymous Njovu (Elephant) Clan final funeral rites event I attended in 2009. On the morning following the first night of the event, close relatives of the deceased gathered in the main house in the courtyard where the rites were taking place and began performing songs that commemorated the life of the deceased. During the performance, a clan *mujjwa* knocked on the door of the house to announce his early arrival. The singers and clappers stopped their performance and answered the door immediately. The one who opened it served the *mujjwa* some of the leftover beer from the previous night's celebrations. The server poured the beer in a gourd with two straws, sipped from one straw first, and then asked the *mujjwa* to sip from the second one. After the *mujjwa* had sipped, the server handed the gourd to him. The *mujjwa* then entered the house. His entrance caused the performers to leave the house while they wept.

This procedure symbolized a rite known as *okwabya olumbe*, literally, "bursting death." The *mujjwa*'s entrance into the house had initiated this rite, and the performers emphasized the rite's importance by raising the volume of their weeping, a reenactment of the way they had cried during the deceased's initial funeral rites. The performers then exited the house with the *mujjwa*, who then stood behind the house door. Here he announced that he had officially taken death out of the house and chased it away: *Twabizza olumbe lw'omugenzi n'ebibamba byonna*—"We have burst the deceased's death and all the sinister spells." He then gave the family of the deceased a go-ahead to install the *musika*, the heir. The *mujjwa* neutralized the gathered participants' intensified expression of mourning, which the performers had highlighted through weeping and exiting the house.

Later in the day the host family served food directly after installing the deceased's heir, a rite known as *okussaako omusika*. During the serving, present *bajjwa* were the only ones who ate meat from the head part of the cow and fish that the family of the deceased had prepared to serve during the event. The family served non-meat eaters caps of the mushrooms they had prepared. These procedures underscored the *bajjwa*'s special power within the Njovu Clan family that hosted the event. After dining, present *bajjwa* performed a joking rite called *okukooza*, in which they rushed into temporary structures called *masanja*—made with dried banana leaves—that gatherers had set up to provide shelter and secure their belongings. Showing off their power, the *bajjwa* attempted to snatch these items while their owners quickly hid them away. Some lost their belongings to the *bajjwa* and had to give them money in order to retrieve the property. During *okukooza*, some *bajjwa* walked from structure to structure, soliciting money from gatherers and dismantling the structures of individuals who were unable to pay. When the final funeral rites ended, the *bajjwa* cleared away all the structures. This procedure signified neutralizing evil forces that many gatherers believed they had left behind in those structures.[42]

These rites speak to the structural role of the *mujjwa* in Buganda. Earlier chapters discussed how the *bajjwa*'s liminality and outsider status among their matrilineal relatives enable them to mediate between the visible and invisible domains. *Bajjwa* individuals may not wield this kind of power among their patriclan relatives because they are insiders in those clans. Conversely, their matrilineal relatives see them as figures with the ability to dispel evil: chasing away death and neutralizing witchcraft, sorcery, and other forces that might threaten the clans' procreative abilities.

Bakaaboobutiko Performers

Wives of Butiko Clansmen, called Bakaaboobutiko, also have official access to Kawuugulu performances. However, they may perform only after having children with their husbands. Aboobutiko believe that when these women bear children, they acquire clan blood through their husbands. Kawere expressed that Butiko Clan blood settles in every clan that has children with Aboobutiko, and that performing with Bakaaboobutiko is one way of tracing, seeking out, and bonding with that blood.[43] Many Kawuugulu members stressed that unless they give birth into the clan, Bakaaboobutiko may not perform with the ensemble, or may perform only in restricted ways. For example, they may approach its drums but may neither touch nor dance to them, as doing so is exclusively for Aboobutiko and the select secondary members of the clan discussed in this chapter. Some Kawuugulu performers stated that their performances may even help validate clan children with or without Butiko Clan blood. According to Nabagereka, if the clan suspects that a wife of a Butiko Clansman acquired a child out of wedlock, members may ask the child in question to dance to the ensemble drums in order to verify the child's clan membership. The clan will determine the membership by the way the drums respond to his or her participation in the performance.[44] Muwagga stated that if a woman is unsure whether her child is a member of the Butiko Clan, she never lets that child perform with Kawuugulu for fear of losing him or her.[45] These customs raise questions about the potential for false incrimination, but they shed light on Kawuugulu's role in managing clan membership in Buganda.

The customs also highlight the importance of procreation as a performative act and the significance of childbearing in Kiganda political life. Gombe told me that when he was growing up in the 1930s, many Baganda who failed to bear children consulted deities to find out why, and to help fix the problem. They feared that dying childless would potentially lead to a forgotten legacy. In the invisible world, spirits of individuals who had produced children teased those of individuals who had been childless. The spirits of childless people often arranged trips to the visible world where they appeared as hissing or nonviolent winds in the bright, midday sunshine. On their arrival they hovered around houses with children that they intended to inspect. When the children came out into their yards, the spirits would wait for a moment when they were quiet. During this moment the spirits bent leaves of banana plants as if they are breaking the leafstalks, planning to claim or take the children who responded to the sounds of the breaking leafstalks. Many parents cautioned their children to stay indoors during the midday sunshine for fear that the jealous spirits might harm them. At times the jealous spirits tormented the parents of the children through dreams and spirit possession, or caused wild animals to visit the victims' homes. Because some spirits of individuals who died childless had the power to torment the living through the property they inherited from them, many people rejected inheritances from such individuals. Given the importance of reproduction among the Baganda, many people historically facilitated reproduction in plants and animals through cross-pollination and mating. Some surviving relatives of the deceased who were exceptionally productive before death indulged in rituals that invoked them, requesting their "reproductive" abilities.[46] Reproduction fosters unity across members of different Kiganda clans, and the participation of Bakaaboobutiko in Kawuugulu events exemplifies this unity. It is another way in which Kawuugulu models and structures political life in Buganda.

Abenvuma Performers

Abenvuma, primary members of the Nvuma (Water Caltrop Seed) Clan, may also take part in Kawuugulu performances because of their historical kin ties to Aboobutiko, and there are multiple stories about these ties. A story told by Katimbo suggests that Abenvuma and Aboobutiko were initially a single clan, the Nvuma Clan, which emerged after the death of its forefather Mulo Wagaba. Following Wagaba's burial, mushrooms grew on his grave. Some clan members interpreted this as Wagaba serving them food and they ate the mushrooms. Others hesitated, since they equated eating the fungi with eating Wagaba. Because of this disagreement, the Nvuma Clan split into two sections. The people who refrained from eating mushrooms, *butiko*, formed the Butiko Clan and declared the mushrooms their primary totem.[47] In this story and many preceding it, kin ties are created as a result of performative actions—such as eating or not eating mushrooms or giving colobus monkey hide—as much as they precede them. Kiganda clan identity can be quite flexible, depending on such acts.

The Kabaka as Performer

Although the *kabaka*—who may come from any clan—rarely performs with Kawuugulu in contemporary times, he is historically an important participant in the ensemble's events, particularly those in royal contexts. Such events serve as spaces where Kawuugulu and the clans that participate in it interact with the *kabaka*. Central to this interaction is the song "Waggongolo Omutanda" (Mr. Millipede the Joiner; see ex. 4.3).

The song features two epithets of the *kabaka*. The first, *Waggongolo*, Mr. Millipede, personifies the millipede as a *kabaka*. Some Baganda believe that the millipede shares some attributes with him, and Kiganda proverbs such as *Togayanga kyezinze*, "Never underestimate that which is coiled," and *N'eggongolo libojja*, "Even a millipede bites," evoke those attributes. The two proverbs—which traditionally caution people who underestimate others or certain things, based on their appearance or behavior—suggest the need for respecting the *kabaka*. Similar to a millipede, he is generally quiet in public, yet

Luganda	English
Waggongolo omutanda,	Mr. Millipede the joiner,
ky'abeeredde,	what he is fond of,
azinga enkata nga tannalaba kya kwetikka.	he rolls a head pad before seeing what to carry.*

*The performers may replace the phrase *azinga enkata nga tannalaba kya kwetikka* with *azinze enkata nga tannalaba kya kwetikka* ("he has rolled a head pad before seeing what to carry") or *atutte entalo nga tannalaba kya kwetikka* ("he has taken wars before seeing what to carry"), both of which share similar rhythmic templates or formulae. The performers may also replace the sub-phrase *kya kwetikka* with *ky'aneetikka* ("what he will carry") or *kya kwebikka* ("with what to cover himself").

Example 4.3. "Waggongolo Omutanda" (Mr. Millipede the Joiner).

he is very powerful. The first proverb evokes the Kiganda practice of equating extreme wealth with a millipede's legs and suggests the *kabaka*'s ability to provide for his subjects.

The second epithet, *omutanda,* "the Joiner," is a derivative of the infinitive *okutanda,* which means "joining parts of a whole together" and/or "creeping up a tree via branches."[48] These interpretations exemplify the high esteem in which all clans in Buganda hold the *kabaka,* whom they recognize as their unifier and overseer, and who may perform with Kawuugulu. Ensemble performers reinforce these meanings by replacing the epithet "the Joiner," with the equally honorific and laudatory label *omukadde,* "elder." Collectively, these epithets reflect how the *kabaka* unites all the clans that participate in Kawuugulu performances and those that Aboobutiko represent before him through such performances, or allow to perform with them in those performances.

According to Kalyemenya, the song "Waggongolo Omutanda" also under-scores the Butiko Clan's freedom to communicate and interact with the *kabaka* informally during Kawuugulu musical events since the reign of Mulondo. Aboobutiko, as the *kabaka*'s maternal relatives, performed for the infant *kabaka* in any way they wanted (described in the preceding chapter). They even danced with their backs turned to him, which is taboo for members of other clans and performance ensembles. This practice, which continues in present times, partly led to those clans nicknaming Aboobutiko *basezi*, a general term for cannibal witches who also engage in esoteric night dancing. The clan's free interactions with Mulondo granted them freedom of expression and interaction before all subsequent *bakabaka*, kings.[49] Aboobutiko's free interactions with the *kabaka* mir-ror those of *bajjwa* with their matrilateral relatives. The interactions partly allow the clan to represent many clans. But as evidenced by blood brotherhood and marriage allied clans that Aboobutiko allow in proximity to Kawuugulu perfor-mances, those clans directly interact with the *kabaka* through such performances. "Waggongolo Omutanda" facilitates these and similar interactions.

Performing Consanguinity

In his 1984 book *A Critique of the Study of Kinship*, David Schneider argued that blood ties are centered on symbols and the meanings that people attach to them. Blood is a culturally defined shared substance that justifies limiting prac-tices to those perceived as relations.[50] The bonds of blood that Aboobutiko share through kinship are only as powerful as they are performed through ritual, narrative, dance, and music. Performance eligibility in Kawuugulu con-firms how blood ties serve as a crucial organizing principle of Kiganda society. Such ties and their associated performance eligibility customs allow ensemble members (Aboobutiko and non-Aboobutiko) to enforce key sociopolitical dis-tinctions that highlight how and why they are linked to the Butiko Clan system. Such management typifies other forms of inter-clan relations and interactions. The sanctions associated with ineligible performance in Kawuugulu are equally central to such relations and interactions as well as clan unity, without which Buganda would be unruly. However, in some cases blood ties alone are insuf-ficient to validate relations between Aboobutiko and any of the other clans that participate in Kawuugulu events; parties from both must have created reciprocal bonds linked to performance. We saw how the construction of some Kawuugulu musical instruments and non-musical performance paraphernalia strengthened an alliance between Aboobutiko and Abengeye. By modeling, structuring, and managing consanguinity, Kawuugulu performance and story-telling exemplify the complex dynamism of Kiganda society and culture.

Chapter Five

Conclusion

A Performative Constitution

In Kawuugulu, musical performance, storytelling, and politics coexist as elements of a whole. Drumming, singing, and dancing work in tandem with human and non-human stories to manage, structure, model, and legitimize power relations in Buganda—to "tune" the kingdom. These power relations involve different actors, whom the ensemble connects and distinguishes. Kawuugulu operates in a sort of equilibrium, mediating kinship, clanship, and kingship in a way that mirrors Kiganda sociopolitical realities. The ensemble's ability to integrate musical performance, storytelling, and politics and to exemplify the overlapping and dialogic nature of these domains make Kawuugulu a performative constitution of polysemic importance (see figure 5.1). By "performative constitution" I mean a constellation of sound and non-sound instruments, songs, dances, and stories through which the ensemble sustains a sociopolitical hierarchy that interweaves and balances kin and clan ties in delicate tension with royal prerogatives. This constitution remains alive as long as Kawuugulu performs, as my analysis of an illustrative event in the following sections will demonstrate.

A Kawuugulu Music and Dance Event

June 8, 2008: I am attending a betrothal, or pre-wedding introduction, ceremony of the daughter of the current Butiko Clan head, the *ggunju*. The young woman is introducing her prospective groom to members of her family, who gather at her father's home in Lugala. The ceremony features a Kawuugulu performance, which opens with a single drummer playing the clan's official *mubala*, a melo-rhythmic pattern with an associated textual phrase, on the *Kijoboje* clan identity drum. The *mubala* goes

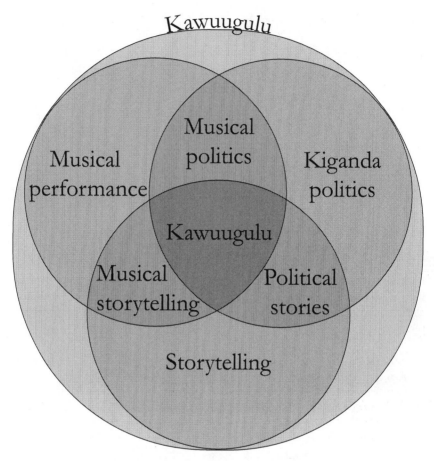

Figure 5.1. The overlapping and dialogic nature of Kawuugulu musical performance, politics, and storytelling.

Weekirikijje; ggunju ajja ("Prepare yourself in joyful anticipation; the *ggunju* is coming"; see ex. 1.1). The performer draws the attention of his audience first by playing initial drum strokes to the accompaniment of a loud yell, *yaaaaa*! He then performs the rhythmic pattern of the *mubala* as he chants its corresponding verbal interpretations. His performance is followed by the first section of Kawuugulu's performance, "Kaaciica," part of which is illustrated in example 5.1.

The player of the ensemble's principal drums, *Kawuugulu* and *Kasajja*, opens "Kaaciica" with rapid drum strokes, which instruct all ensemble members to prepare for their individual performance roles. The various drummers of the ensemble then start making their entries into the section in a way that reflects the hierarchy of their drums, from highest to lowest: the *Nyamitongo* drum pair; the *Kawuugulu* and *Kasajja* drum pair; the *Nyoolaevvubuka* drum; and the *mpuunyi* drum. *Nyamitongo's* player enters "Kaaciica" with a drumbeat called "Nnamulondo" (example 5.1, measure 1; the drumbeat is discussed in chapter 3). The beat's ostinato-like style helps regulate the ensemble's performance tempo. The *Nyamitongo* drummer accompanies this beat with its associated text and varies his rhythmic pattern only slightly as the performance progresses (measures 12 and 16).

Next, the *Kawuugulu* and *Kasajja* drummer enters with his first beat, "Gwa" (Prostrate; end of measure 1). The drummer accompanies the beat with its associated text, and varies his rhythmic pattern in the course of the performance (measures 12 to 23).

Although the *Nyoolaevvubuka* drum has a higher status than the *mpuunyi* drum, the players of both drums make their initial entries into the "Kaaciica" section at the same time (measure 3). Unlike the *Kawuugulu* and *Kasajja* and the *Nyamitongo* drum pairs, the *Nyoolaevvubuka* drum plays a syncopated musical part that emphasizes and elaborates on the beats of other drums in Kawuugulu. This part adds tonal and rhythmic complexity to the ensemble's music. Conversely, the player of the *mpuunyi* drum sounds a steady pulse (measures 3 to 23) that serves as the central beat of the music, regulating the performance tempo and helping dancers keep their footwork in time to the music. Overall, the *mpuunyi* drummer's part holds Kawuugulu's dense polyrhythmic texture together.

After all of the drummers have made their entries into the first section, the *Kawuugulu* and *Kasajja* drum part gradually grows louder (measure 5). This change in dynamics signals the lead dancer of the ensemble to launch the first dance. The rest of the dancers then join him in performing his pattern, which involves lifting and lowering the legs in alternate fashion. Simultaneously, the lead dancer introduces the first song, "Waggongolo Omutanda" (Mr. Millipede the Joiner), shortly after launching the first dance (end of measure 6). Then the rest of the ensemble joins in performing the song in a call-and-response style (measure 8). Meanwhile, the pellet bells that the dancers wear on their ankles produce a simple rhythmic pattern (measures 6–11) when the performers start dancing. This pattern changes slightly, with variations that the lead dancer initiates within the various dances (measures 12–21 and 22–23).

The subsequent dance involves the performers occasionally shuffling their feet on the ground and jerking the upper parts of their bodies as spirits possess them. Initially, the dancers perform in a circular configuration around the drums, but as they modify their movements, they spread out across the performance arena. Eventually they return to the circular formation, this time lifting their legs higher and keeping their heads upright, probably to avoid becoming dizzy. This dance concludes the first section of the ensemble performance.

To usher in the second section of Kawuugulu, "Waggongolo," which takes its name from the "Waggongolo Omutanda" song, the player of the *Kawuugulu* and

Kasajja drums performs a very loud variation of the "Gwa" beat on the pair. The second section is slower, and the ensemble's reduced tempo allows the dancers to relax a bit after the intense performance of the first section. They start out by shuffling their feet on the ground as they dance in a circle around the Kawuugulu drum set. Then they dance while wiggling their waists and lifting their feet slightly from the ground in alternation and landing on the balls of their feet. For the most part, the drummers maintain their drumbeats from the first section. However, the ensemble performs many different songs, making the second section of the performance the most elaborate and extensive one. Each song takes its initial cue from a rhythmic pattern of the ensemble's chief drums, *Kawuugulu* and *Kasajja*. Sometimes the ensemble performs call-and-response parts with the drum pair's beats. These exchanges confirm how Kawuugulu drums communicate like humans, with humans. Later on, the call-and-response exchanges occur between a soloist and the ensemble's chorus.

Again using the "Gwa" beat, the *Kawuugulu* and *Kasajja* player leads the ensemble into the third and closing section of the performance, "Okugaba" ("Sharing"), the name of the dance that concludes Kawuugulu events. It is the fastest and most complex and energetic section of the three. In this section the drummers generally maintain their basic drum parts from the previous two sections, but they perform them faster. The complex musical dialogue of the performers' drum and dance rhythms, coupled with the climactic and exciting nature of the section, make it difficult to discern all that I hear in its dense musical texture. The dancers jump very high, kick vigorously, and undergo intense spirit possession while the *Kawuugulu* and *Kasajja* drummer plays rhythms that accentuate their choreography. Near the conclusion of the performance, the dancers engage in a performance of "Sharing": They pair up, each facing his or her partner up close, and then have verbal exchanges about sharing as every dancer holds on tightly to his or her companion's hands. The couples also make high leaps while scissoring their legs in the air, following which they land on the ground with gusto and mutual excitement. Many performers describe this formation as expressing unity and as one that allows them to "share" the dance with each other and with the absent *kabaka*, as if inviting him to join them. Each couple performs the dance several times, prolonging the third section of the performance and making it the longest of the three. Like many Kawuugulu events, this occasion demonstrates the interconnectedness of musical performance, storytelling, and politics.

Musical Performance, Politics, and Storytelling

Kawuugulu storytelling in the illustrative event integrates human and non-human stories in a multimodal fashion, fusing songs, dances, instruments, and

Example 5.1. First section of a Kawuugulu performance, "Kaaciica."

Example 5.1.—*(continued)*

Example 5.1.—*(continued)*

Example 5.1.—*(continued)*

Example 5.1.—*(continued)*

Example 5.1.—*(concluded)*

myriad objects, all of them rich with symbolism.[1] Human stories include the oral accounts that inform the various aspects of the ensemble. These narratives document Kawuugulu's history, validate its political currency, bolster the historical legitimacy of Kawuugulu performers, offer performance guidelines, and act as a framework for handling the ensemble's items. The accounts highlight Kawuugulu's multiple origins. Thus, variant versions of a single story serve as separate stories, each providing an explanation that contributes an individual perspective to the ensemble's "official" narrative in an accretive fashion. No single account contains all the details about the ensemble. These divergent accounts mirror Kawuugulu's musical texture, which draws on multiple drumbeats, songs, and dances, and its multidimensional importance (political and musical). Through this diversity, primary members of the Butiko Clan, Aboobutiko, and their ensemble are able to represent many clans before the *kabaka* and to encompass multiple principles of kinship, clanship, and kingship.

Drum beats, songs, and dances also recount stories. Like the oral narratives that inform Kawuugulu's practice, the ensemble's repertoire is diverse in meaning. For example, the opening solo performance of the Butiko Clan *mubala* on the *Kijoboje* drum narrates important clan history. It reenacts the practice of the *ggunju* announcing his arrival at the court of Ssekabaka Mulondo (r. ca. 1524–54) and that of the *kabaka* preparing to welcome him and other Aboobutiko in his company (described in chapter 3). But the *mubala* also signals the presence of the *ggunju* at the betrothal, or pre-wedding introduction, ceremony in question and his approval of the ensemble's participation in the event.

Similarly, the *Nyamitongo* drum pair's drumbeat "Nnamulondo" expresses many of the stories discussed in chapter 3. It recalls the mutual relationship between Aboobutiko and the *kabaka* in addition to celebrating Ssekabaka Mulondo's mother, Nnamulondo, for raising him. In addition, the drumbeat validates the Kiganda throne, *Nnamulondo*, which takes its name from Mulondo's mother. *Kawuugulu* and *Kasajja's* drumbeat "Gwa" communicates to the *kabaka's* subjects the necessity to honor him through prostrating. But the beat also memorializes the historical support that Ssekabaka Kintu (r. ca. beginning of the fourteenth century) received from the Butiko Clan to recapture power in Buganda. "Gwa" legitimizes Aboobutiko's centuries-old relationship with royalty and signifies the *kabaka's* relationship with other clans, as well. Similarly, through the "Waggongolo Omutanda" song, Aboobutiko express their free interactions with the *kabaka*, his ability to lead and unite all clans in Buganda, and the clan's willingness to serve him. Also cautioning ineligible performers about the dangers of performing with Kawuugulu, the song legitimizes the Butiko Clan's royal privileges, confirming that Aboobutiko and their Kawuugulu Ensemble stand in for all clans in the ensemble vis-à-vis the *kabaka*.

The various songs or chants featured in the second section of the event also commemorate historical kinship between Aboobutiko and primary members of other clans through descent, marriage, and blood brotherhood alliances (discussed in chapter 4). Other songs celebrate the *ggunju*'s historical role in developing and overseeing many of the Kawuugulu events discussed in chapter 2. Also, the dance "Okugaba," which concludes the third section of the performance, allows the ensemble to "share" Kawuugulu dances with each other and the *kabaka*. The movement is a reenactment of Aboobutiko's historical and official intimacy with Ssekabaka Mulondo and later leaders of Buganda (discussed in chapter 3). Since every Kiganda clan has a special relationship with the *kabaka* through at least one official hereditary duty, this dance also demonstrates how the Aboobutiko's closeness to him constitutes the core of relations between all clans and the *kabaka* in Buganda. Not only the Kawuugulu Ensemble but also Aboobutiko and all clans are in a sense twinned with the *kabaka*, for he could come from any one of them.

As is the case in many parts of Africa, music and dance historically share a dual relationship among the Baganda.[2] The complementarity of music and dance in the illustrative event highlights the ensemble's performance practice as one that centers on the notion of twinning or doubling, a theme that is omnipresent in Kiganda society. The male is often twinned with the female, the visible with the invisible, the living with the dead, the royal with the commoner, the primary with the secondary, and the present with the past, among other binary relationships. The twinned relationship between Kawuugulu music and dance, the pairing of the *Kawuugulu* and *Kasajja* drums, and other ensemble practices model this ubiquitous concept of duality. Because it encompasses Kawuugulu, the ensemble expresses these forms of twinning. Kawuugulu also twins musical performance and storytelling, allowing the ensemble to sustain the political web of kinship, clanship, and kingship. Thus, Kawuugulu is a model for and embodiment of multiple forms of twinning.

The betrothal event also models the various clan and royal settings in which many Baganda associated with Kawuugulu manage political interactions, and it speaks volumes about these interactions. The settings include the clan-based contexts discussed in chapter 1: child initiations and confirmations, twin initiations, weddings, final funeral rites, installations of leaders, recitations of genealogies of the clan's various lineages, official meetings, and gatherings during which Aboobutiko learn more about each other. Most of these occasions apply to all clans in Buganda. The incorporation of Kawuugulu into the occasions within the Butiko Clan illustrates the ensemble's broad relevance and role in signifying different dynamics of Kiganda clan politics.

Kawuugulu also performs at official occasions involving the *kabaka*, whom ensemble members entertain and protect as part of Aboobutiko's hereditary obligations to him and the whole Kiganda kingship. Kawuugulu performances in royal contexts enable the ensemble to stand in for and represent many clans before the *kabaka*. For instance, Aboobutiko often perform with primary members of other clans, particularly those with whom they have close blood ties. Moreover, because every clan has its own duty or more to perform for the *kabaka*, Aboobutiko's obligations to protect and entertain him through Kawuugulu dramatize those duties. Kawuugulu's various contexts serve as spaces in which performers and their audiences reinforce the sociopolitical hierarchy that draws on kingship, clanship, and kingship. The historian Neil Kodesh writes of the interconnectedness of these domains, a relationship that allows them to serve as the framework for intra-clan politics, royal politics, and inter-clan politics in the Kiganda society.[3]

The relationships of the ensemble's performers and audience members also tell stories about the sociopolitical hierarchy in which these actors exist. Given Aboobutiko's hereditary ownership of Kawuugulu, they are the chief official performers in the ensemble. With the clan's permission, primary members of other clans with strong blood ties to the clan through descent, marriage, and blood brotherhood, among other connections, perform with the ensemble. These performers include Abengeye (primary members of the Ngeye Clan), Abenvuma (primary members of the Nvuma Clan), Bakaaboobutiko (wives of Butiko Clansmen), and *bajjwa* (clanswomen's children) of Aboobutiko.

The Butiko Clan reinforces these arrangements by reminding all attendants that Kawuugulu's drums have supernatural power capable of killing or incapacitating ineligible performers—individuals with no clan blood—who attempt to play the drums and sing and dance to them. Through managing performance eligibility the ensemble "distinguishes," "embraces," and "excludes" and otherwise regulates members of the Kiganda society.[4] It connects and separates members of different clans on the basis of blood ties, while ensuring that the clans are united under the *kabaka*. The performer-audience dynamics and identities that Kawuugulu embodies help sustain hierarchy across Buganda's sociopolitical strata. Performance eligibility in the ensemble also is evidence of the relative flexibility of Kiganda consanguinity, a relativity that is at the heart of the intra-clan and inter-clan politics that Kawuugulu structures and models.

These dynamics in turn shape the ensemble's musical meaning, while being shaped by it. The ethnomusicologist Denis-Constant Martin writes, "Musical meaning . . . is not inscribed in the intrinsic characteristics of music, but is assigned through dialogic processes involving, in particular circumstances, producers and receivers."[5] This definition of "musical meaning" characterizes the Kawuugulu performance process. Not all Kawuugulu actors are human. The ensemble's musical instruments and performance paraphernalia and the various practices associated with these items contribute to the agency through non-human storytelling (that supplements human storytelling). Kawuugulu drums have personal names, life, and supernatural qualities. Accordingly, these drums speak and sing like their human players, who treat them as relatives, ancestors, spirits, and kings. The performers feed, dress, and make requests to them. They also carefully observe the various customs associated with the instruments' construction, use, and maintenance. The instruments have a private house, a fact that has broader political implications.

Historically, every household head constructed a round shelter made of mud, timber, woven strands of papyrus, and reeds, thatched with grass (similar to a Kawuugulu traditional house). High-profile Baganda hired servants to build their houses, and these structures featured polished reeds, a marker of high status, that set these houses apart from those of ordinary people. The reeds were used to construct various parts of the shelter, including posts, walls, ridges, rafters, and roof beams. These houses also had more elaborate designs than those outside the palace. The weaving of their papyrus strands was more intricate. Each structure had a principal coil that was bigger than the rest of its strands. Above the entrance and around the door frame of the house stood more reeds that were tied together. The dwelling's roof rested on a central pillar consisting of rafters bound together.[6] Thus, a Kiganda house expressed hierarchy and power relations.

Generally, a house's roof (kasolya) is a symbol for a clan head (owaakasolya) and a clan's unity. Its interior represents Abeekika (clan members). In other words, a Kiganda clan and its various hierarchical levels and lineages are comparable to a house, with clan members bound together in the same structure as the clan head. The relationship is one of mutual interdependence. The relationship between the words for "roof" and "clan head" suggest that clan members depend on the clan head for protection. But he also depends on them for support.

This arrangement mirrors the relationship between the clans and the kabaka, who is to Aboobutiko and their Kawuugulu Ensemble as the Kingdom of Buganda is to all clans, and as a clan head is to clan members. The encompassing of Kawuugulu under the kabaka is important because it simultaneously affirms each clan head's authority by association with royalty. Consequently, the house is a model of the Kiganda clan organization and monarchy, in which the kabaka acts as the roof and the clans as the interior. Also, as discussed in the introduction, the house is the most basic unit of the Kiganda clan administrative structure.[7] Many events that serve as the backbone of sociopolitical interactions in Buganda take place in or depend on the existence of the house. Similar to the ritual of reciting genealogies (okulanya), the custom of storing Kawuugulu in a house of its own underscores these principles and arrangements.

Another practice that sheds light on the meaning of the ensemble's house is the use of a basket (kibbo) in the Kawuugulu events. In the first chapter I describe how ensemble members and some of their audience members place monetary alms (bigali) in this basket to request blessings or give thanks to the ancestral spirits associated with the ensemble. These baskets (bibbo) have wider meanings than just being receptacles. In Buganda, the strands that a woman weaves together to make a basket signify relatives. The woven strands of a basket are like the woven roof of the house, symbolizing the relatives that make up a family.

Gombe stated that when wives make loose baskets, their husbands' clans point to the poor craftsmanship as a cause of "loose" relationships within their families. While there may be other causes of such relationships, this belief reinforces an important traditional responsibility of a Muganda wife in her home: to weave tight baskets.[8] Kawuugulu's basket is a visual reminder of this responsibility and the important role wives play in mediating relations across different clans. Ensemble performances weave close relations among many clans related through descent, marriage, and brotherhood. Kawuugulu's basket, which also allows ensemble members and their audiences access to Butiko Clan ancestral spirits, is an important marker of these arrangements.

The symbolism of other forms of performance paraphernalia featured in the Kawuugulu illustrative event also tells stories that are integral to sociopolitical meanings. The *Kawawa* royal spear that never leaves the ensemble drums represents Ssekabaka Nakibinge (r. ca. 1494–1524). Without it, Kawuugulu and its royal identity are incomplete. The colobus monkey (*ngeye*) fur belts that dancers tie around their waits represent primary members of the Ngeye Clan and its primary totem. These accessories highlight the closeness of the group to the Butiko Clan. Similarly, the sheepskin bands that the dancers wrap around their ankles before tying pellet bells around them and the sheepskin laces that they use to fasten the bells, collectively signify primary members of the Ndiga Clan and their primary clan totem. The use of sheep (*ndiga*) skin accessories in Kawuugulu also affirms the historically close relationship between primary members of the Butiko and Ndiga Clans. The sounds of the dancers' bells help summon spirits that possess them during performance, allowing Kawuugulu to mediate the natural and supernatural worlds. The ethnomusicologist David Coplan writes, "Performance expression . . . emerges as an aspect of social action and resonates with emotion and meaning among members of communities inscribed in social ideology and practice."[9] Citing the anthropologist Edward Schieffelin, the ethnomusicologist Veit Erlmann echoes Coplan's words: "Performance . . . is an 'emergent social construction' whose efficacy and meaning are created in the relationship between social actors."[10] These observations apply to Kawuugulu, as the foregoing discussion suggests.

Furthermore, because the ensemble's actors include human and non-human performers, its performance expression draws on, and is a form of, storytelling. Every aspect of Kawuugulu tells a story—from the oral accounts that inform its performances and actions of the human performers, to the agency and symbolism of musical instruments and other forms of performance paraphernalia, to the way the performers treat these items as kin and ancestors. The multimodality of Kawuugulu stories helps structure social interactions and define political meanings. The stories help explicate a theory or discourse of performance practice that is as musical as it is political, as familial as it is social, as palpable as it is invisible in its consequences and importance. Musical performance and storytelling collectively allow the ensemble to encompass, express, and shape principles of kinship, clanship, and kingship. Accordingly, it mediates different forces, including male and female, visible and invisible, life and death or living and dead, relatives and ancestors, royals and commoners, primary and secondary, present and past, and wakefulness and sleeping. Kawuugulu is an embodied and performative model of and for these principles and their associated power relations.[11]

Appendix A

Glossary

This glossary contains Luganda words and a few key non-Luganda terms as they are used in this volume.

aba *prep. pl.* of; *v.* is

abaamasiga *n. pl.* primary clan lineage heads (title)

Abateregga, Bateregga *n. pl.* royal lineage of reigning kings

Abeekika *n. pl.* clan members

abeemituba *n. pl.* secondary clan lineage heads (title)

abeeredde *v.* "she/he is fond of"

abempya *n. pl.* quaternary clan lineage heads (title)

Abengeye *n. pl.* primary members of the Ngeye Clan

abennyiriri *n. pl.* tertiary clan lineage heads (title)

abennyumba *n. pl.* quinary clan lineage heads (title)

Abenvuma *n. pl.* primary members of the Nvuma Clan

abina *v.* "she/he is dancing while jumping and raising legs very high"

aboobusolya *n. pl.* "ones constituting roofs"; clan heads (title)

Aboobutiko *n. pl.* primary members of the Butiko Clan

aga *prep. pl.* of

agaligenda *v. pl.* "which will go"

ajja *v.* "she/he is coming"

aka *adj.* of

akademe *n.* academy

akali *v.* "that which is"

akugoba *v.* "one who chases you" or "one who is chasing you"

Akugoba *n.* name of a drum-making workshop

alifumbirwa *v.* "she/he will be cooked for" (she/he will get married)

alikatunda *v.* "she/he will sell it"

Amaganda *adj.* of or relating to the Baganda

Amaggunju *n.* "dances associated with the *ggunju*"; cover term for Kawuugulu dances

amala *v.* "one who finishes"; "one who completes"; "one who averts"

aneetikka *v.* "she/he will carry"

Ankole, Nkole, Nkore *n.* interlacustrine Bantu kingdom in southwestern Uganda
asula *v.* "she/he who dwells"
atudde *v.* "you who is seated"
atutte *v.* "she/he who has taken"
avaayo *v.* "whoever comes from there"
azinga *v.* "she/he rolls up"
azinze *v.* "she/he has rolled up"
b' *prep. pl.* of
ba *prep. pl.* of
baakisimba *v.* "they planted it"
Baakisimba *n.* cover term for a music and dance genre
baalyanga *v. pl.* "they used to dine"
baana, *a*baana *n. pl.* children
Baanabaakintu *n. pl.* "children of Kintu" (descendants of Kintu)
babinyi, *a*babinyi *n. pl.* "jumpers" or "raisers"
Babinyi, Ababinyi *n. pl.* cover term for Kawuugulu dancers
badongo, *a*badongo *n. pl.* group of musicians
Badongo, Abadongo *n. pl.* court or palace ensemble comprising lyre, fiddle, flute, rattle, and drum players
Baganda, Abaganda *n. pl.* natives of Buganda
bagezi, *a*bagezi *n. pl.* sages; gods; deities (title)
baggunju *n. pl.* Butiko Clan heads (title)
bajjajja *n. pl.* grandfathers; grandmothers; great-uncles; great-aunts; forefathers; ancestors
bajjwa, *a*bajjwa *n. pl.* clanwomen's children; sisters' children
Bakaaboobutiko *n. pl.* wives of Butiko clansmen
bakabaka *n. pl.* kings (title)
bakadde, *a*bakadde *n. pl.* elders
bakkojja *n. pl.* maternal uncles
bakongozzi, *a*bakongozzi *n. pl.* spirit mediums (title)
bakulembeze, *a*bakulembeze *n. pl.* leaders
balabirizi, *a*balabirizi *n. pl.* custodians or caretakers (title)
balamuzi, *a*balamuzi *n. pl.* judges (title)
baleezi, *a*baleezi *n. pl.* drum makers/tuners (title)
balogo, *a*balogo *n. pl.* witches
balongo, *a*balongo *n. pl.* twins
banaabibba *v. pl.* "they will probably rob them [the plump or dumb ones]"
banaakubba *v. pl.* "they will probably rob you"
Bannabuddu *n. pl.* residents of Buddu County
Bannabusiro *n. pl.* residents of Busiro County
Bannaggunju *n. pl.* dancers of Amaggunju
Bannakyaddondwa *n. pl.* residents of Kyaddondo County
Bantu *n. pl.* group of people and/or languages
basezi, *a*basezi *n. pl.* cannibal witches
basika, *a*basika *n. pl.* heirs; heiresses
bassekabaka, basekabaka *n. pl.* deceased kings (title)

bassenga *n. pl.* father's sisters; paternal aunts
bataka, *a*bataka *n. pl.* clan heads; owners of permanent places of residence
Bayegga *n.* one of the *masiga* of the Butiko Clan
bazireegera *v. pl.* "they tune them from/for"
bazzukulu *n. pl.* grandchildren; descendants
bbali *adv.* aside
bbiri *adj.* two
be *prep. pl.* of
Bemba *n.* name of fearless fighter, allegedly a snake
bibamba, *e*bibamba *n. pl.* misfortunes; calamities; sinister spells
bibanja, *e*bibanja *n. pl.* plots of land
bibbo, *e*bibbo *n. pl.* baskets
bifa, *e*bifa *v. pl.* "matters that concern/pertain to"; about
bigali, *e*bigali *n. pl.* alms
bijja, *e*bijja *n. pl.* clan or family burial sites
bika, *e*bika *n. pl.* clans
bikuzzi, *e*bikuzzi *n. pl.* fur belts for dancing
binyumu, *e*binyumu *n. pl.* parties; festivities
bita, *e*bita *n. pl.* gourds
bitabo, *e*bitabo *n. pl.* books
bitanyi, *e*bitanyi *n. pl.* placentas
bitono, *e*bitono *pron. pl.* little; "the little"
biwonvu, *e*biwonvu *n. pl.* valleys
biwuugulu, *e*biwuugulu *n. pl.* owls
budde, *o*budde *n.* time
bufumbo, *o*bufumbo *n.* marriage
Buganda *n.* interlacustrine Bantu kingdom in south-central Uganda
bugere *n. pl.* small feet; small toes
bukedde *v.* "it is morning/dawn"
bukojja, *e*bukojja *n.* maternal side
Bulange *n.* Buganda's administrative building/headquarters
buli *adj.* every; each
bulijjo *adj.* ordinary; regular
bulira *n. pl.* umbilical cords
Bunyoro, Nyoro *n.* interlacustrine Bantu kingdom in southwestern Uganda
Bugoga, Soga *n.* interlacustrine Bantu kingdom in southeastern Uganda
busolya *n.* roofs
butagaba, *o*butagaba *adv.* "not sharing"
butaka, *o*butaka *n.* clan or historical estate(s); permanent place(s) of residence
butiko, *o*butiko *n. pl.* mushrooms (*Termitomyces microcarpus*)
butwe, *o*butwe *n. pl.* small heads
bw' *rel. adv.* when; if
bwakabaka, *o*bwakabaka *n.* kingship
bwe *conj.* when; if
bya *prep. pl.* of.
byakedde *v. pl.* "they [dumb/plump ones] arose early"

byazze *v. pl.* "they [the plump/dumb ones] came"
byonna *adj. pl.* "all of them"
ddala *adv.* indeed
e *prep.* at
era *conj.* as well as; also; and
evvubuka *n.* "the stalwart youth"
ewa *adv.* "at the home of"
ey' *adj.* of
eya *prep.* of
eyasooka *adj.* "the first one"
eyitibwa *verb.* "it is called"
ez' *prep.* for
eza *prep. pl.* of
ezaatuwonya *v. pl.* "those which saved us from"
ezeebase *v. pl.* "those which are sleeping"
ezitunula *v. pl.* "those which are awake"
federo *n.* federalism
ffumbe, effumbe *n.* civet cat
galiba *v. pl.* "they will be"
-ganda *adj.* stem signifying cultural aspects of the Baganda
Ganda *adj.* descriptor for cultural norms and practices of the Baganda
ggabogabo, eggabogabo *n.* three-quarter shape
ggongolo, eggongolo *n.* millipede
ggunju *n.* Butiko Clan head (title)
ggw' *rel. pron.* you
gusinga *v.* "is better than"
gw' *prep.* of
gwa *v.* prostrate
gwonna *adj.* "the entire"; "all of it"
gyakyo *adj.* "its"
gye *adv.* where
jjajja *n.* grandfather; grandmother; granduncle; grandaunt; forefather
ka *v.* let; allow (short form of *leka,* "let")
Kaaciica *n.* first movement of a contemporary Kawuugulu's performance
kabaka *n.* king from the Bateregga or Abateregga royal lineage (title)
Kabanda *n.* one of the *mituba* of the Butiko Clan
kabbiro, akabbiro *n.* secondary totem
kadinda, akadinda *n.* seventeen-to-twenty-one-key xylophone
Kadinda, Akadinda *n.* name of a court or palace ensemble
kaliba, akaliba *n.* small hide
kalira, akalira *n.* umbilical cord
kamanyibwa *v.* "it is known by"
kasajja *n.* "small man"
Kasajja *n.* large, twin, male drum of the Kawuugulu instrument set
kasolya, akasolya *n.* roof
kasujja *n.* Ngeye Clan head (title)

katikkiro *n.* prime minister (title)
katiko, akatiko *n.* mushroom (*Termitomyces microcarpus*)
Kato *n.* name of a young male twin
katinvuma, akatinvuma *n.* type of creeper (plant)
Kawawa *n.* royal spear of the Kawuugulu instrument set
kawuugulu, akawuugulu *n.* "small owl"
Kawuugulu *n.* large, twin, female drum of the Kawuugulu instrument set; cover term for a clan-royal music and dance ensemble
Kawuula *n.* ancestral spirit and/or deity; head of the Mujaguzo Drums of Kingship (title)
kayingo *adj.* outstanding
kazze *v.* "it has come"
kibanja, ekibanja *n.* plot of land
kibbo, ekibbo *n.* basket
kibiina, ekibiina *n. pl.* organization; association; class
Kiganda *adj.* descriptor for cultural norms and practices of the Baganda
Kijoboje *n.* "Mumble the text"; name of the Butiko Clan's identity drum
kika, ekika *n.* clan
Kikwerudde *n.* name of a royal drum
Kireezi *n.* official tuner and repairer of royal drums (title)
Kiryankolo *n.* famine period during which people survived on rhizomes
kita, ekita *n.* gourd
kitabo, ekitabo *n.* book
kitanyi, etitanyi *n.* placenta
kiwuugulu, ekiwuugulu *n.* owl
kkanzu, ekkanzu *n.* loose-fitting tunic(s) made from silk, cotton, poplin, or linen
kkobe, ekkobe *n.* air potato (*Dioscorea bulbifera*)
kkojja *n.* maternal uncle
kkubo, ekkubo *n.* road; way
Koki *n.* kingdom in southwestern Uganda incorporated within Buganda in 1896
ku *prep.* on; about; *conj.* when
kubina, okubina *v.* "to dance while jumping and/or raising legs very high"
Kubina, Okubina *n.* one of the cover terms for Kawuugulu dances and dancing style
kuboneka, okuboneka *v.* to appear
kugaba, okugaba *v.* "to share"; "to serve"; "to apportion"
Kugaba Okugaba *n.* name of a Kawuugulu dance; closing section or movement of a Kawuugulu performance
kugejja, okugejja *v.* to fatten
kugula, okugula *v.* to buy
kukooza, okukooza *n.* joking rite involving *bajjwa* and their maternal kin
kulannama, okulannama *v.* to sit with legs stretched forward
kulanya, okulanya *v.* to recite genealogies of the clan lineages
kuleega, okuleega *v.* to tune; to tension; to stretch
kulya, okulya *v.* to eat
kumanyagana, okumanyagana *v.* getting to know each other better
Kumbagara *n.* name of a royal drum

kumbika, okumbika *v.* "to announce my death"
kunaga, okunaga *v.* to play initial musical parts
kusamira, okusamira *v.* to invoke ancestral spirits to possess the invokers
kussaako, okussaako *v.* to install
kutabaala, okutabaala *v.* "to wage war for"; to go to war
kuva, okuva *prep.* from; since
kuyimba *v.* to sing or chant
kuyitibwa, okuyitibwa *v.* to be called
kw' *prep.* of
kwa *prep.* of
kwabya, okwabya *v.* "to burst" (to send away)
kwalula, okwalula *v.* "to hatch" (to initiate and confirm)
kwawula, okwawula *v.* "to divide"; "to split"; "to partition"
Kwawula, Okwawula *n.* name of a Kawuugulu dance
kwebikka okwebikka *v.* to cover oneself
kwefuga, okwefuga *v.* to be independent
kwetikka, okwetikka *v.* to carry
ky' *prep.* of
kya *pron.* "that which to"
kye *prep.* of
Kyebabona *n.* name of a royal drum
kyezinze *pron.* "that which is coiled"
lannama *v.* "sit with your legs stretched forward"
libojja *v.* "it bites"
lubiri *n.* palace or royal enclosure
lubu *n.* relation; sibling; line
lubugo, olubugo *n.* bark cloth
luganda, oluganda *n.* kinship; brotherhood
Luganda, Oluganda *n.* native language of the Baganda
lugave, olugave *n.* pangolin
luggya *n.* courtyard; quaternary clan lineage
lukato, olukato *n.* awl
luyimba *n.* song or chant
Lukiiko, Olukiiko *n.* parliament
Lukwata *n.* name of a deity
lulimi, olulimi *n.* language; tongue; dialect
lumbe, olumbe *n.* death
lunyiriri *n.* line; tertiary clan lineage
lutalo, olutalo *n.* war; battle; debate
lw' *prep.* of
lwa *prep.* of
lwo *pron.* yours
lwomwa *n.* Ndiga Clan head (title)
maaso, amaaso *n. pl.* face(s); eyes
mabega, emabega *n.* rear; behind
makabi, amakabi *n. pl.* prongs

maliba, *a*maliba *n. pl.* animal hides

mannya, *a*mannya *n. pl.* names

masanja, *a*masanja *n. pl.* dried banana leaves; temporary shelters made from dried banana leaves

masaza, *a*masaza *n. pl.* counties

masiga, *a*masiga *n. pl.* hearthstones; primary clan lineages

masiro, *a*masiro *n. pl.* tombs

mata, *a*mata *n.* milk

matongo, *a*matongo *n.* "desolation following calamity"; "calamity in dejection"; "calamity in disparity"

matooke, *a*matooke *n. pl.* bananas

matume. *a*matume *n.* "that which is sent"; message

mawuugulu, *a*mawuugulu *n. pl.* large owls

mbaga, *e*mbaga *n.* wedding(s); feast

mbogo, *e*mbogo *n.* buffalo

Mbogo *n.* name of a drum-making workshop

mbugo, *e*mbugo *n. pl.* bark cloths

mibala, *e*mibala *n. pl.* drum melo-rhythmic patterns with associated textual phrases

miko, *e*miko *n. pl.* transpositions

minyolo, *e*minyolo *n. pl.* drumsticks; beaters

mirembe, *e*mirembe *n.* peace

mirimu, *e*mirimu *n. pl* duties; responsibilities; jobs; tasks

mirugwa, *e*mirugwa *n. pl.* cavities; shells

misambwa, *e*misambwa *n. pl.* type of spirits and/or deities

miseetwe, *e*miseetwe *n. pl.* plains

mituba, *e*mituba *n. pl.* fig trees (*Ficus natalensis*); secondary clan lineages

miziro, *e*miziro *n. pl.* primary clan totems

mmamba, *e*mmamba *n.* lungfish

mmandwa, *e*mmandwa *n.* type of a spirit and/or deity

mmere, *e*mmere *n.* food

mpeewo, *e*mpeewo *n.* oribi or bush (gray) duiker

mpisa, *e*mpisa *n.* customs

mpologoma, *e*mpologoma *n.* lion

mpuunyi, *e*mpuunyi *n.* "hummer"; "moaner"; name of a medium-sized conical drum of the Kawuugulu instrument set

mpya *n.* courtyards; quaternary clan lineages

mu *prep.* in

mubala, *o*mubala *n.* drum melo-rhythmic pattern with an associated textual phrase

mudingidi, *o*mudingidi *n.* tube-fiddle player

Muganda, *O*muganda *n.* native of Buganda

mugema *n.* Nkima Clan head (title)

mugenzi, *o*mugenzi *n.* deceased

mugezi, *o*mugezi *n.* sage (title); god; deity

Mujaguzo *n.* Royal Drums of Kingship

mujjwa, *o*mujjwa *n.* clanwoman's child; sister's child

mukadde, *o*mukadde *n.* elder (title)

mukago, omukago *n.* blood brotherhood
mukazi, omukazi *n.* woman
mukonda, omukonda *n.* "handle"; mushroom stem or base
mukongozzi, omukongozzi *n.* spirit/deity medium (title)
mukulu, omukulu *n.* head; leader (title)
mulabirizi, omulabirizi *n.* custodian (title)
mulangira, omulangira *n.* prince (title)
muleezi, omuleezi *n.* drum maker/tuner (title)
Mulembe, omulembe *n.* reign
mulongo *n.* twin; double
mulonzi, omulonzi *n.* "picker" (finder)
mulwanirizi, omulwanirizi *n.* defender
Mulyabyaki *n.* "Why do you eat them?"; name of a royal drum
Munnaggunju *n.* "dancer of Amaggunju"
muno *adv.* "in here"
munyolo, omunyolo *n.* drumstick; beater
musaayi, omusaayi *n.* blood
musajja, omusajja *n.* man
musigire, omusigire *n.* deputy (title)
musiige, omusiige *n.* court/palace page (title)
musika, omusika *n.* heir; heiress
mutaka, omutaka *n.* clan head (title); owner of a permanent place of residence
mutanda, omutanda *n.* "joiner"; *kabaka*'s epithetic title
mutuba, omutuba *n.* fig tree (*Ficus natalensis*); secondary clan lineage
mutuuze, omutuuze *n.* resident owner of a permanent place of abode
Muwawa *n.* former name of the Kingdom of Buganda
muzigo, omuzigo *n.* ghee
muziro, omuziro *n.* primary clan totem
mwana, omwana *n.* child
mwe *adv.* "in which we"
mwenge, omwenge *n.* beer
mwezi, omwezi *n.* moon
n' *conj.* and; as well as
na *conj.* and; as well as
Nalubaale *n.* Luganda name for Lake Victoria
namasole *n. kabaka*'s mother (title)
Namitongo *n.* name of the small drum pair of the Kawuugulu instrument set
nyoola *v.* "twist"
namuyama *v.* "I welcomed him/her"
namwama *n.* Kkobe Clan head (title)
ndege, endege *n.* metallic pellet bells
ndere, endere *n. pl.* twisted animal hide cords
ndi *v.* "I am"
ndiga, endiga *n.* sheep
ndingidi, endingidi *n.* tube-fiddle
ndongo, endongo *n.* bowl-lyre

nduli, enduli *n.* trunk(s); stump(s); stem(s)

ne *conj.* and

Nende *n.* name of an ancestral spirit and/or sage

nga *conj.* "it is likely"; "as they will"; when

ngabi, engabi *n.* bushbuck

ngeye, engeye *n.* colobus monkey

ngo, engo *n.* leopard

Nilo-Hamites *n.* group of people and/or languages

Nilotes *n.* group of people and/or languages

Njagalakweetikka *n.* "I want to carry"; name of a royal drum

njala, enjala *n.* hunger

njogera *v.* "I speak"

njovu, enjovu *n.* elephant

nju *n.* house(s)

njulu *n.* type of herb (*Marantochloa*)

nkata, enkata *n.* head pad; wreath

nkima, enkima *n.* monkey

nkolo, enkolo *n.* rhizome(s)

nkolwa, enkolwa *n.* mongoose

nkondo, enkondo *n.* stake

nkula, enkula *n.* rhinoceros

nkulaakulana, enkulaakulana *n.* development

nkuluze, enkuluze *n.* dictionary

nkya *n.* morning

Nkyeru *n.* name of a god

Nnaalongo *n.* title name of a mother of twins

Nnamulondo *n.* name of Buganda's kingship throne; woman's name

nnamulondo *n.* type of mushroom

nnanga, ennanga *n.* bow-harp

nneekirikijje *v.* "flaunt myself in joyful anticipation"

nnono, ennono *n.* customs; norms

nnyabo *n.* mother; madam

nnyaabwe *n.* "their mother" or "their maternal aunt"

nnyiriri lines; tertiary clan lineages

nnyoko *n.* "your mother"

nnyumba *n.* house(s); quinary clan lineage(s)

nsaanikizo, ensaanikizo *n.* [mushroom] cap

nsawo, ensawo *n.* amniotic sac(s)

nseka *v.* "I laugh"

nsi, ensi *n.* nation; country

Nsigadde *n.* "I have stayed"; name of Kawuugulu's hereditary *ssenga*; originally, human arm-bone beater of the Kawuugulu and Kasajja drum pair

nsimbi *n.* cowry shell(s)

nsonga, ensonga *n.* reason(s); purpose(s)

nsozi, ensozi *n. pl.* mountains

nsuku, ensuku *n. pl.* plantations

nswaswa *n.* monitor lizard
ntalo, entalo *n. pl.* wars
ntebe, entebe *n.* stool; chair
nvubu, envubu *n.* hippopotamus
nvuma, envuma *n.* water coltrap seed (*Trapa natans*)
ny-, nny- *n.* "mother of"
Nyamitongo *n.* name of the small drum pair of the Kawuugulu instrument set
nyoola *v.* "twist"
Nyoolaevvubuka *n.* "Twist the stalwart youth" or "Wrestle down the stalwart youth";
 name of the single-headed, long drum of the Kawuugulu instrument set
oba *conj.* or
ogutegeeragana *v.* "that which gets along"
ogw' *adj.* of
okaggira *v.* "you pluck it from"
okaggya *v.* "you uproot it"
okutuuka *prep., conj.* until
olugenda *v.* "that which leaves"
olwa *prep.* of
omuliraano *n.* neighborhood
omulwanyammuli *n.* "one who fights with reeds"; title of Ssekabaka Nakibinge
Omuteesa *n.* "Muteesa's [reign]"
omwa *prep.* in
ondabe *v.* "for you to see me"; "for you to give me your attention"
otudde *aux. v.* "you are seated/sitting"
ow' *adj.* of
owaakasolya *n.* "one constituting the roof" (clan head's title)
owennyumba *n.* quinary clan lineage head (title)
owessiga *n.* primary clan lineage head (title)
owooluggya *n.* quaternary clan lineage head (title)
owoolunyiriri *n.* tertiary clan lineage head (title)
owoomutuba *n.* secondary clan lineage head (title)
oyinze *aux. v.* "you are able"
ozze *aux. v.* "you have come"
Ruhuuga *n.* original name, from Bunyoro, of Ssekabaka Kintu
si *adv.* not; "it is not"
sikyomu *n.* "it is not for a single person"
Sikyomu *n.* name of a drum-making workshop
ssaabaganzi *n.* "father of all beloved"; "greatest of all"; honorable title of the Butiko
 Clan
ssaabataka *n.* "most supreme *mutaka*"; "father of all *bataka*" (king's, *kabaka*'s, title)
ssaalongo *n.* title name of a father of twins
ssekabaka *n.* deceased *kabaka*
ssenga *n.* paternal aunt; father's sister
Ssese *n.* islands in Lake Victoria
ssiga, essiga *n.* hearthstone; primary clan lineage
ssiro, essiro *n.* tomb

Sudanic *n.* group of people and/or languages

tannalaba *aux. v.* "she/he has not seen yet"

talwa *aux. v.* "she/he does not take long"

tattibwa *v.* "she/he is not killed"

tebaabibbe? *v.* "will they not rob them?"

tebaakubbe? *v.* "will they not rob you?"

teludda *v.* "it never returns"

temuli *v.* "there [inside] isn't any"

teva *v.* "from there does not come"

togayanga *v.* "never underestimate"

Toro *n.* interlacustrine Bantu kingdom in southwestern Uganda

tositama *v.* "do not squat"

ttaka, ettaka *n.* land; soil

twabeeranga *v.* "we used to reside at"

twabizza *v.* "we have burst"

twalyanga *v.* "we used to eat"

Vvamuluguudo *n.* "Get out of the road"; name of a royal drum

w' *adj.* of

wa *prep.* of; for

Waggongolo *n.* "Mr. Millipede"; name of the second movement of a contemporary Kawuugulu performance; *kabaka*'s epithetic title

walukagga *n.* head of royal blacksmiths (title)

weekirikijje *v.* "prepare yourself in joyful anticipation"

y' "is the one who"

ya *adj.* of; for

yaakyo *adj.* "its"

yaaaaa! *excl.* expression of affirmation

yaaye! *excl.* "oh my!"

yekka *adj.* alone

za *adj.* of

zaago *pron.* theirs

zaatuwonya *v.* "they saved us from"

zaffe *pron.* our(s)

ze *pron.* "are the ones which"

zivugira *v.* "they sound for"; "they sound from" "they sound at"

Zinga *n.* name of an island

ŋŋoma, eŋŋoma *n.* drum(s)

Appendix B

Author Interviews

Listed here are the individuals I interviewed who are referenced throughout the book. Interviews were conducted in Luganda and recorded in high-definition format using a Sony HD/ HDR-SR10 video camera and in wave format using a Sony PCM-D50 audio recorder. I photographed them with a Canon Rebel XTI camera. I am currently working with the Butiko Clan to archive all my recordings at the clan estate in Bukalango. For each interview listed I provide the interviewee's name, starting with the clan name; year of birth; primary clan membership; connection to Kawuugulu (where applicable); occupational or administrative title(s); occupation(s); date of interview; and the name of the village or town and district where I conducted the interview. For English translations of clan names, see list on p. 2.

Binywera, Erasmus Kyagaba. Born 1933. Butiko Clan member, Kawuugulu dancer, and farmer. Interviewed July 18, 2008, Bumbajja village, Mukono District.

Bbirikkadde, Francis. Born 1934. Butiko Clan member, Kawuugulu performer and dance trainer, and primary school teacher. Interviewed July 19, 2008, Kituuza village, Mukono District.

Ganaayaba, Ignatio Kawere. Born 1919. Butiko Clan member, Kawuugulu performer, secondary clan lineage head, and farmer. Interviewed July 19, 2008, Kaalengeera village, Mukono District.

Gombe, Kabenge. Born 1931. Butiko Clan member, Kawuugulu performer, choir conductor, retired lecturer, historian, linguist, Kabaka Foundation official, primary subclan lineage deputy head, secondary clan lineage head, consultant with Luganda Language Association, president of Luganda Authors' Association, board member of Lubiri Secondary School, and secretary of Volunteer Promoters of Church Music Association. Interviewed August 4, 2008, August 25, 2009, and December 9, 2010, Namirembe town, Kampala District.

Kalyemenya, George William. Born 1940. Butiko Clan member, Kawuugulu performer, and preacher. Interviewed August 2, 2008, Bukalango village, Wakiso District.

Kasiga, Diriisa. Born 1969. Butiko Clan member, Kawuugulu drummer, and electrical technician. Interviewed August 5, 2008, Kasubi town, Kampala District.

Kasirye, Mike. Born 1943. Butiko Clan member, Kawuugulu performer, retired primary school head teacher, and businessman. Interviewed August 5, 2008, Kaabuwambo-Busuubizi-Kinene village, Mityana District.

Katimbo, Bulasio. Born 1958. Butiko Clan member, Kawuugulu performer, tertiary clan lineage head, and businessman. Interviewed July 19, 2008, Kikoona village, Mukono District.

Kavuma, Umaru Mukasa. Born 1942. Ngo Clan member, Kawuugulu dancer, and farmer. Interviewed June 16, 2008, Kaliiti village, Wakiso District.

Kawere, Matia. Born 1946. Butiko Clan member, Kawuugulu performer, twenty-fifth Butiko Clan head, retired civil servant, motor vehicle mechanic, merchandise transporter, and farmer. Interviewed August 5, 2008, Lugala town, Kampala District.

Kawere, Pius Sempa. Born 1929. Butiko Clan member, Kawuugulu performer, and magistrate. Interviewed July 26, 2008, Namwezi village, Mukono District.

Kinene, Peter. Born 1969. Lugave Clan member and secondary school fine art and Luganda teacher. Interviewed June 22, 2009, Buwagga village, Wakiso District.

Ntudde, Maria Luiza. Born 1916. Butiko Clan member, Kawuugulu performer, and farmer. Interviewed June 16, 2008, Bukalango village, Wakiso District.

Lutwama, George. Born 1929. Butiko Clan member, Kawuugulu performer, and farmer. Interviewed July 18, 2008, Kisoko village, Mukono District.

Matovu, Deziderio Kiwanuka. Born 1924. Ngabi Clan member, father of twins, former tube-fiddle player in the Badongo ba Kabaka Court Ensemble (king's lyre, fiddle, flute, rattle, and drum players), and proprietor and director of the Badongo Dancers performing group. Interviewed June 7, 2008, and August 15, 2008, Nakawuka, Wakiso District.

Maviirinkata, Jamaada. Born 1947. Butiko Clan member, Kawuugulu performer and dance trainer, and farmer. Interviewed July 25, 2008, Buziika village, Mukono District.

Mugwanya, Hannington Joshua Kizza. Born 1956. Butiko Clan member, Kawuugulu performer, entrepreneur, and farmer. Interviewed July 19, 2008, Kisoga village, Mukono District.

Mulondo. Born 1953. Anonymous clan membership. Prince, medium of Ssekabaka Mulondo's spirit, and overseer of Ssekabaka Mulondo's tomb. Interviewed August 1, 2008, Bulondo-Mitweebiri village, Wakiso District.

Musiitwa, Herbert Mulasa Bbirikkadde. Born 1957. Butiko Clan member, Kawuugulu Ensemble custodian, retired senior police officer, security officer of the *kabaka*, and executive director of Pearl Childcare Initiative–Uganda. Interviewed July 26, 2008, Entebbe town, Wakiso District.

Muwaga, Charles Lutaaya. Born 1924. Butiko Clan member, Kawuugulu performer, father of twins, retired civil servant, and farmer. Interviewed July 25, 2008, Nsenge village, Mukono District.

Muwagga, Anthony Mugagga. Born 1966. Butiko Clan member and professor of education at Makerere University. Interviewed August 4, 2008, Namugongo town, Wakiso District.

Ng'anda, Yisaaya. Born 1943. Butiko Clan member, Kawuugulu performer and farmer. Interviewed July 19, 2008, Ntakafunvu village, Mukono District.

Nabagereka, Brenda Najjuka. Born 1944. Butiko Clan member, Kawuugulu performer, page in Ssekabaka Cwa I's palace, and chef. Interviewed July 30, 2008, Kireka town, Wakiso District.

Najjuka, Annet. Born 1946. Butiko Clan member and Kawuugulu performer. Interviewed August 5, 2008, Kaabuwambo-Busuubizi-Kinene village, Mityana District.

Nakibinge. Date of birth unknown. Anonymous clan membership, medium of Ssekabaka Nakibinge's spirit and overseer of Ssekabaka Nakibinge's tomb. Interviewed August 1, 2008, Bubinge-Kongojje village, Wakiso District.

Nakitto, Yozefiina. Born 1929. Ngeye Clan member, Kawuugulu performer, and farmer. Interviewed June 16, 2008, Bukalango village, Wakiso District.

Nakyagaba, Costa. Born 1971. Butiko Clan member, Kawuugulu performer, and nursery school teacher. Interviewed July 18, 2008, Bumbajja village, Mukono District.

Nalugunju, Goreti. Born 1982. Butiko Clan member, Kawuugulu performer, and farmer. Interviewed July 18, 2008, Bumbajja village, Mukono District.

Nsereko, Yesoni. Born 1928. Kkobe Clan member and retired secondary school and college instructor in Luganda, music, and handicrafts. Interviewed July 7, 2009, Lungujja-Kikandwa town, Kampala District.

Semugooma, Fredrick Kaggwa. Born 1951. Butiko Clan member, Kawuugulu performer, and automobile technician. Interviewed August 2, 2008, Busega town, Kampala District.

Sensonga, Muhammad. Born 1928. Butiko Clan member, Kawuugulu performer, father of twins, primary clan lineage head, spirit medium, and retired civil servant. Interviewed July 26, 2008, Kawotto village, Wakiso District.

Sebuwuufu, Simeo Ssemmambo. Born 1959. Njovu Clan member, instrument maker, multi-instrumentalist, former player of the seventeen-to-twenty-one-key xylophone in the Kadinda Court Ensemble, and instructor of traditional music and instrument making at Kyambogo University. Interviewed June 23, 2009, Kigoowa town, Kampala District.

Wagaba, Steven. Born 1917. Butiko Clan member and retired civil servant. Interviewed July 24, 2008, Lubaga town, Kampala District.

Walakira, Francis. Born 1971. Mbogo Clan member, instrument maker, entrepreneur, director of St. Francis Junior School, and owner of Akugoba Drum Makers and Mbogo Drum Producers. Interviewed August 15, 2008, Mpambire town, Wakiso District.

Notes

Acknowledgments

1. The Ugandan villages and towns where I did fieldwork are Banda, Bubinge-Kongojje, Bukalango, Bukeerere, Buligi, Bulondo-Mitwebiri, Bumbajja, Busega, Busoke, Buteregga-Mitwebiri, Buwagga, Buwambo, Buziika, Buziranduulu, Entebbe, Gavu, Ggaba, Kaabuwambo-Busuubizi-Kinene, Kaalengeera, Kaaliiti, Kabigi, Kagganda, Kakeeka, Kamwookya, Kasubi, Katadde, Katende, Katwe, Kawempe, Kawotto, Kigoowa, Kigulu, Kikoona, Kireka, Kirinnya, Kisagazi, Kisoga, Kisoko, Kisozi-Kiyoola, Kituuza, Kiwango-Bukeerere, Kyambogo, Kyengera, Lubaga, Lugala, Lungujja-Kikandwa, Lusaze, Lutengo-Naggalama, Makerere, Mataba, Matugga, Mpambire, Mpereerwe, Nakasero, Nakawuka, Nakirama, Nakisunga, Namirembe, Namugongo, Namwezi, Nateete, Nansana, Nsenge, Ntakafunvu, Ntinda, and Vumba-Kiwangula.

Note on the Musical Examples

1. See Katamba and Cooke 1987.
2. For further use of the term "open tone," see Wilcken 1992.

Preface

1. For a detailed discussion of "entextualization," see Richard Bauman and Charles L. Briggs 1990.
2. Thanks to my late maternal great-uncle Kabenge Gombe (1931–2016), who facilitated this access and served as a significant resource for integral information regarding the ensemble, including its historical, sociocultural, and political aspects. Gombe was a Kawuugulu drummer, primary member of the Butiko Clan, deputy head of a primary clan lineage (*owessiga omusigire*), head of a secondary clan lineage (*owoomutuba*), choir conductor, retired lecturer, historian, and linguist.
3. This saying could also be translated as "The drums do not sound where they are made."

4. "Interlactusrine" means "between lakes"—in this case the lakes are the Great Lakes of East Africa, including Lakes Victoria and Tanganyika. Besides Buganda, the other four kingdoms are the southeastern Kingdom of Busoga (historically a multikingdom state) and the southwestern Kingdoms of Ankole, Bunyoro, and Toro. The demographics of the five kingdoms are part of a larger group of sub-Saharan Bantu-speaking societies. In Uganda, these societies historically occupy the southern part of the country. In addition to Bantu speakers, other major linguistic groups occupy Uganda. They include Nilotes (traditionally in the north-west), Nilo-Hamites (in the north-central area), and Sudanic speakers (in the northeast). Unlike Bantu-speaking societies, the demographics of these groups are historically segmentary, "with authority vested in chiefs from noble clans who have territorial rights and who exert their authority over people of other clans who reside on their land" (Anderson 1968, 17). These linguistic groups and their members have distinct cultural norms and practices that define their identities beyond geographical demarcations.
5. Odhiambo, Ouso, and Williams 1977, 52.
6. This story was told by Kabenge Gombe.
7. Gombe, interview by author, December 9, 2010.
8. Nannyonga-Tamusuza 2005, 10.
9. Gombe, interview by author, August 4, 2008.
10. Odhiambo, Ouso, and Williams 1977, 52–56.
11. Ward 1991.
12. Ibid.
13. Ward 1998, 411.
14. Kodesh 2010, 3. For further perspectives on Kiganda history, kingship, and politics, see Wrigley 1996; Kizza 2010; Kodesh 2010; Nannyonga-Tamusuza 2005; Stephens 2013; Thomson 2016.
15. Ward 1998, 411.
16. Ibid., 412.
17. Ibid.
18. Ibid.
19. Ray 1991, 116.
20. Ibid., 5.
21. Ibid., 116.
22. Ibid., 117–18.
23. The foregoing account is based on Tumusiime 1997, 55–72.
24. Ssemakula, Mukasa, "The Territory of Buganda," http://www.buganda.com/masaza.htm; accessed November 26, 2017.

Introduction

1. Gombe, interview by author, December 9, 2010.
2. Muwagga, interview by author, August 4, 2008.

3. The clan is also historically in charge of thatching shelters in the *kabaka*'s palace, a duty that relates directly to his status as the roof (*kasolya*) of the kingdom; the duty offers a symbolic reference that binds clan loyalties across domains of duty.

4. For a similar discussion of ritual theory and practice, see Bell 2009, 57.

5. Chernoff 1979, 34.

6. Kaminski 2012, 1.

7. Kruger 2007, 36.

8. The inextricable nature of these domains is evident in the way the ensemble articulates and embodies them through its performance practice.

9. Many scholars have discussed oral history, myth, and storytelling at length in Buganda and beyond. See Wrigley 1996; Philips 2005; Finnegan 2007; Keller and Kuautonga 2007; Mushengyezi 2007; Kizza 2010; Kodesh 2010; Fleisch and Stephens 2016.

10. Howard 2014, xii.

11. For further discussion of this subject and an interpretation of oral traditions about fishery in Central Africa, see Gordon 2016, 50–51.

12. Kawere, interview by author, July 26, 2008.

13. Katimbo, interview by author, July 19, 2008.

14. Mugwanya, interview by author, July 19, 2008.

15. Finnegan 2015, 134.

16. Anonymous interviewee, Namirembe town, Kampala District.

17. On the use of the term "invented tradition," see Hobsbawm and Ranger 1992.

18. Kafumbe 2004, 2006.

19. Kasirye, interview by author, August 5, 2008.

20. Semugooma, interview by author, August 2, 2008.

21. Sensonga, interview by author, July 26, 2008.

22. Kalyemenya, interview by author, August 2, 2008.

23. Nalugunju, interview by author, July 18, 2008.

24. Nsimbi published the book in 1956.

25. Gombe, interview by author, August 4, 2008.

26. Every deceased *kabaka* (*ssekabaka*, pl. *bassekabaka*) has a spirit medium, called *mukongozzi*, who communicates between the dead and the living. The spirit mediums, *bakongozzi*, of *bassekabaka* are of a much higher status than *bakongozzi* of other kinds of spirits.

27. Nakibinge, interview by author, August 1, 2008.

28. Nannyonga-Tamusuza 2005, 36.

29. Wagner 1977, 623.

30. Matovu, interview by author, June 7, 2008.

31. Turner 1967, 1969.

32. Turner 1969, 95.

33. Kinene, interview by author, June 22, 2009.

34. For a discussion of the mother's brother in South Africa, see Radcliffe-Brown 1952.

35. Matovu, interview by author, June 7, 2008.

36. See Roscoe 1911; Kagwa 1934, 1952; Fallers 1960; Nsobya 2000.

37. See Kagwa 1949; Nsimbi 1956; Buteraba 1990; Ttendo 2002.
38. See Kiwanuka 1971, 1972; Kagwa 1971; Mawanda 1999; Kasirye 1959; Wavamunno 2004, 2007; Ssekamwa 2001, 2007; Kiwalabye 2008; Kasozi 2013.
39. See Sempebwa 2004; Muwanga 2005; Kirega-Gava 2006.
40. See Lush 1935; Wachsmann 1953, 1971; Anderson 1968, 1984; Cooke 1970, 1992, 1996; Kubik 1960, 1964, 1968, 1969; Gray 1998; Makubuya 1995, 1999, 2000; Nannyonga-Tamusuza 2005; Nattiez and Nannyonga-Tamusuza 2005.
41. Lévi-Strauss 1969.

Chapter One

1. Merriam 1964, 45.
2. Cries of animals such as leopards, hyenas, and wild dogs have also historically indicated some form of impeding calamity, but many people take cries of owls very seriously due to their association with death. Lyrics such as *Kawuugulu kazze, obudde bukedde* ("Small owl has come, the time has come") and *Galiba mawuugulu agaligenda okumbika* ("They will be big owls that will go announce my death") document the owl's association with death and highlight the Kiganda practice of using diminutive and augmentative pronouns to refer to important things.
3. For more information on these ensembles, see Anderson 1968 and Cooke 1996.
4. See Nakazibwe 2005 for more information about the importance of bark cloth in Buganda.
5. Mukasa, interview by author, July 28, 2005.
6. Walakira, interview by author, August 15, 2008.
7. Gombe, interview by author, December 9, 2010.
8. Mulondo, interview by author, August 1, 2008.
9. Muwagga, interview by author, August 4, 2008.
10. Ntudde, interview by author, June 16, 2008.
11. Gombe, interview by author, August 4, 2008.
12. Wagaba, interview by author, July 24, 2008.
13. Sensonga, interview by author, July 26, 2008.
14. Kasiga, interview by author, August 5, 2008.
15. Gombe, interview by author, December 9, 2010.
16. Ibid.
17. Ibid.
18. Muwagga, interview by author, August 4, 2008.
19. Binywera, interview by author, July 18, 2008.
20. Muwaga, interview by author, July 25, 2008.
21. Musiitwa, interview by author, July 26, 2008.
22. Wagaba, interview by author, July 24, 2008.
23. Musiitwa, interview by author, July 26, 2008.
24. Sensonga, interview by author, July 26, 2008.

25. Musiitwa, interview by author, July 26, 2008.
26. Nakyagaba, interview by author, July 18, 2008.
27. Ganaayaba, interview by author, July 19, 2008.
28. See chapter 4 for an ethnographic description of a Kawuugulu performance.

Chapter Two

1. Nakitto, interview by author, June 16, 2008.
2. See, for instance, Lush 1935, 12; Nsimbi 1956, 234.
3. The species is *Termitomyces microcarpus.*
4. Gombe, interview by author, August 4, 2008.
5. Ibid.
6. Ibid.
7. The theme of human sacrifice exists only in centuries-old mythology and not in more recent discourse.
8. Gombe, interview by author, August 4, 2008.
9. Kawere, interview by author, August 5, 2008.
10. Muwagga, interview by author, August 4, 2008.
11. Kasiga, interview by author, August 5, 2008.
12. Gombe, interview by author, August 4, 2008.
13. Gombe, interview by author, August 4, 2008.
14. Gombe, interview by author, August 4, 2008.
15. Kalyemenya, interview by author, August 2, 2008.
16. Bbirikkadde, interview by author, July 19, 2008.
17. Gombe, interview by author, August 4, 2008.
18. Gombe, interview by author, August 9, 2010.
19. Kinene, interview by author, June 22, 2009.
20. Gombe, interview by author, August 9, 2010.
21. For a discussion of Kiganda names and their origins, see Nsimbi 1956.
22. Fallers 1960, 53.
23. Sebuwuufu, interview by author, June 23, 2009.
24. Nabagereka, interview by author, July 30, 2008.
25. Matovu, interview by author, June 7, 2008.

Chapter Three

1. Muwaga, interview by author, July 25, 2008.
2. Ganaayaba, interview by author, July 19, 2008.
3. Sensonga, interview by author, July 26, 2008.
4. Pryor (2007) writes, "The djelis, sometimes known as griots, are a hereditary caste of musicians and singers, once closely connected to the royal court, whose vast repertoire of praise songs, genealogies, oral histories and more constitute the living memory of Mali's Mande-speaking people" (42–43). In West

Africa, griots are often seen as leaders because of their use of words laden with hereditary meanings to shape society.

5. Kulubya (1942, 49–56) notes that *Kyebabona* was a small drum that came with Kintu to Buganda, but was burned, probably during one of the early wars.
6. Gombe, interview by author, December 9, 2010.
7. Ibid.
8. Ibid.
9. Lush 1935, 14.
10. Gombe, interview by author, December 9, 2010.
11. Nsereko, interview by author, July 7, 2009.
12. *Amatongo* can also be translated as "calamity in wilderness," "calamity in dejection," or "calamity in disparity."
13. Gombe, interview by author, August 4, 2008.
14. Ibid.
15. Kalyemenya, interview by author, August 2, 2008.
16. Kyagaba, interview by author, July 30, 2008.
17. Sensonga, interview by author, July 26, 2008.
18. Mujuuli, interview by author, July 21, 2008.
19. Kasirye 1959, 12.
20. Lutwama, interview by author, July 18, 2008.
21. Ganaayaba, interview by author, July 19, 2008.
22. Nabagereka, interview by author, July 30, 2008.
23. Roscoe 1911, 217–18.
24. Kasirye 1959, 12.
25. Ganaayaba, interview by author, July 19, 2008.
26. Kawere, interview by author, July 26, 2008; Lutwama, interview by author, July 18, 2008.
27. Semugooma, interview by author, August 2, 2008.
28. Nsimbi 1956, 211.
29. Sensonga, interview by author, July 26, 2008.
30. Kagwa 1949, 54.
31. Kalyemenya, interview by author, August 2, 2008.
32. Semugooma, interview by author, August 2, 2008.
33. Nakyagaba, interview by author, July 18, 2008.
34. Muwagga, interview by author, August 4, 2008.
35. Gombe, interview by author, August 25, 2009.
36. Kagwa 1971, 21–23.
37. Gombe, interview by author, August 25, 2009. See also Nsimbi 1956 for another version of this story.
38. Ganaayaba, interview by author, July 19, 2008.
39. Semugooma, interview by author, August 2, 2008.
40. Muwagga, interview by author, August 4, 2008.
41. Ganaayaba, interview by author, July 19, 2008.
42. Gombe, interview by author, August 4, 2008.
43. Ibid.
44. Kalyemenya, interview by author, August 2, 2008.

45. Kasirye 1959, 12; Nsimbi 1956, 234; Lush 1935, 12.
46. Kasirye 1959, 12.
47. Gombe, interview by author, August 4, 2008.
48. Charry 2000.
49. Nsimbi 1956, 211.
50. Nsimbi 1956, 211–13.
51. Ibid., 213–14.
52. Kagwa 1949, 54–55.
53. Kagwa 1971, 23.
54. Kasirye 1955, 12.
55. Gombe, interview by author, August 4, 2008.
56. Ibid.
57. Gombe, interview by author, December 9, 2010.
58. Nsobya 2000, 54–56.
59. Bbirikkadde, interview by author, July 19, 2008.
60. Lutwama, interview by author, July 18, 2008.
61. Kalyemenya, interview by author, August 2, 2008.
62. Gombe, interview by author, December 9, 2010.
63. Musiitwa, interview by author, July 26, 2008.
64. Kasiga, interview by author, August 5, 2008.
65. Sensonga, interview by author, July 26, 2008.
66. Katimbo, interview by author, July 19, 2008.
67. Kalyemenya, interview by author, August 2, 2008.
68. Ng'anda, interview by author, July 19, 2008.
69. Lutwama, interview by author, July 18, 2008.
70. Maviirinkata, interview by author, July 25, 2008. Nende is a sage that the clan allegedly consulted before making some Kawuugulu drums and their associated paraphernalia; Kawuula is also the title name for the head of the Mujaguzo Drums of Kingship.
71. Mujuuli, interview by author, July 21, 2008.

Chapter Four

1. Nalugunju, interview by author, July 18, 2008.
2. Kasiga, interview by author, August 5, 2008.
3. Najjuka, interview by author, August 5, 2008.
4. See Gidal (2014, 84) on the discussion of the terms "distinguish," "exclude," and "embrace" as I use them here.
5. Nabagereka, interview by author, July 30, 2008.
6. This title could also be translated as "greatest of all beloved."
7. Gombe, interview by author, July 19, 2008.
8. Kalyemenya, interview by author, August 4, 2008.
9. Kalyemenya, interview by author, August 2, 2008
10. Kasirye, interview by author, August 5, 2008.

11. Gombe, interview by author, August 4, 2008.
12. Ibid.
13. Kalyemenya, interview by author August 2, 2008.
14. Katimbo, interview by author, July 19, 2008.
15. Nalugunju, interview by author, July 18, 2008.
16. Sensonga, interview by author, July 26, 2008.
17. Muwaga, interview by author, July 25, 2008.
18. Mugwanya, interview by author, July 19, 2008.
19. Sensonga, interview by author, July 26, 2008.
20. Kawere, interview by author, August 5, 2008.
21. Ng'anda, interview by author, July 19, 2008.
22. Gombe, interview by author, August 4, 2008. For more discussions of land and politics in Africa, see Hanson 2003; Sackeyfio-Lenoch 2014; Gordon 2016.
23. Gombe, interview by author, August 4, 2008.
24. Ganaayaba, interview by author, July 19, 2008.
25. Ibid.
26. Other meanings of Okwawula are "Splitting," Sharing," and "Separating."
27. Nakitto, interview by author, June 16, 2008.
28. Gombe, interview by author, August 4, 2008.
29. Kawere, interview by author, August 5, 2008.
30. Roscoe 1911, 19.
31. Fallers 1960, 56.
32. Kagwa 1934, 135.
33. Fallers 1960, 56.
34. Nsobya 2000, 56.
35. Kagwa 1934, 135.
36. Kinene, interview by author, June 22, 2009.
37. Muwaga, interview by author, July 25, 2008.
38. Sahlins 2011, 2.
39. Kavuma, interview by author, June 16, 2008.
40. Ibid.
41. Binywera, interview by author, July 18, 2008.
42. I must maintain confidentiality regarding some of the details of this occasion.
43. Kawere, interview by author, August 5, 2008.
44. Nabagereka, interview by author, July 30, 2008.
45. Muwagga, interview by author, August 4, 2008.
46. Gombe, interview by author, December 9, 2010.
47. Katimbo, interview by author, July 19, 2008.
48. Kiingi 2007, 551.
49. Kalyemenya, interview by author, August 2, 2008.
50. Schneider 1984.

Chapter Five

1. For a discussion of the term "multimodal" as I use it here see Finnegan 2007.

2. See Nannyonga-Tamusuza 2005, 21.
3. Kodesh 2010, 6.
4. On the discussion of the terms "distinguish," "exclude," and "embrace," as I use them here, see Gidal (2014, 84).
5. Martin 2013, 48–49.
6. Gombe, interview by author, August 4, 2008.
7. See also the notions of the "house society," introduced by Lévi-Strauss (1982) and refined by Carsten and Hugh-Jones (1995) and Joyce and Gillespie (2000).
8. Gombe, interview by author, August 4, 2008.
9. Coplan 2008, 5.
10. Erlmann 1991, 5 (citing Schieffelin 1985, 721).
11. On the use of the terms "embodied" and "performative" see Vasquez 2011.

Works Cited

Anderson, Lois Ann. 1968. "The *Miko* System of Kiganda Xylophone Music." PhD diss., University of California, Los Angeles.

———. 1984. "Multi-part Relationships in Xylophone and Tuned-Drum Traditions in Buganda." In *Selected Reports in Ethnomusicology, Volume 5: Studies in African Music*, edited by J. H. Kwabena Nketia and Jaqueline Cogdell DjeDje, 121–41. Los Angeles: University of California, Los Angeles Department of Ethnomusicology.

Bauman, Richard, and Charles L. Briggs. 1990. "Poetics and Performance as Critical Perspectives on Language and Social Life." *Annual Review of Anthropology* 19: 59–88.

Bell, Catherine. 2009. *Ritual Theory, Ritual Practice*. New York: Oxford University Press.

Buteraba, Lawrence. 1990. *Ekika ky'e Ngabi ne Nnono Yaakyo* [The Bushbuck Clan and its history]. Kampala: Akademe y'Oluganda.

Carsten, Janet, and Stephen Hugh-Jones. 1995. *About the House: Lévi-Strauss and Beyond*. Cambridge: Cambridge University Press.

Charry, Eric S. 2000. *Mande Music: Traditional and Modern Music of the Maninka and Mandinka of Western Africa*. Chicago: University of Chicago Press.

Chernoff, John Miller. 1979. *African Rhythm and African Sensibility: Aesthetics and Social Action in African Musical Idioms*. Chicago: University of Chicago Press.

Cooke, Peter. 1970. "Ganda Xylophone Music: Another Approach." *African Music* 4 (4): 62–80, 95.

———. 1992. "Report on Pitch Perception Experiments Carried out in Buganda and Busoga (Uganda)." *African Music* 7 (2): 119–25.

———. 1996. "Music in a Uganda Court." *Early Music* 24 (3): 439–52.

Coplan, David B. 2008. *In Township Tonight!: South African Black City Music & Theatre*. Chicago: University of Chicago Press.

Curzon. 2009. "The Constituent Kingdoms of Uganda." *ComingAnarchy* (blog), March 13, 2009. http://cominganarchy.com/2009/03/13/the-constituent-kingdoms-of-uganda.

Erlmann, Veit. 1991. *African Stars: Studies in Black South African Performance*. Chicago: University of Chicago Press.

Fallers, Margaret Chave. 1960. "The Eastern Lacustrine Bantu (Ganda, Soga)." In *Ethnographic Survey of Africa: East Central Africa*, pt. 11, edited by Daryll Forde. London: International African Institute.

Finnegan, Ruth H. 2007. *Hidden Musicians: Music-Making in an English Town*. Middletown, CN: Wesleyan University Press.

Fleisch, Axel, and Rhiannon Stephens. 2016. *Doing Conceptual History in Africa.* Oxford: Berghahn Books.

Geertz, Clifford. 1973. *The Interpretation of Cultures.* New York: Basic Books.

———. 1993. "Religion as a Cultural System." In *The Interpretation of Cultures: Selected Essays*, rev. ed., 87–125. London: Fontana Press.

Gidal, Marc M. 2014. "Musical Boundary-Work: Ethnomusicology, Symbolic Boundary Studies, and Music in the Afro-Gaucho Religious Community of Southern Brazil." *Ethnomusicology* 58 (1): 83–109.

Gordon, David M. 2016. *Nachituti's Gift: Economy, Society, and Environment in Central Africa.* Madison: University of Wisconsin Press.

Gray, Catherine T. 1998. "Static and Dynamic Codes in Kiganda Lyre Song." *Contemporary Music Review* 17 (3): 7–14.

Hanson, Holly Elisabeth. 2003. *Landed Obligation: The Practice of Power in Buganda.* Portsmouth, NH: Heinemann.

Hobsbawm, Eric, and Terence Ranger, eds. 1992. *The Invention of Tradition.* New York: Cambridge University Press.

Howard, Keith. 2014. Preface to *Theory and Method in Historical Ethnomusicology*, edited by Jonathan McCollum and David G. Hebert, ix–xiii. New York: Lexington Books.

Joyce, Rosemary A., and Susan D. Gillespie, eds. 2000. *Beyond Kinship: Social and Material Reproduction in House Societies.* Philadelphia: University of Pennsylvania Press.

Kafumbe, Damascus. 2004. "The Continuity and Change of the Nnanga among the Baganda People of Central Uganda." Unpublished paper, Makerere University, Kampala.

———. 2006. "The Kabaka's Royal Musicians of Buganda-Uganda: Their Role and Significance during Ssekabaka Sir Edward Frederick Muteesa II's Reign (1939–1966)." MA thesis, Florida State University, Tallahassee.

———. 2011. "The Kawuugulu Royal Drums: Musical Regalia, History, and Social Organization among the Baganda People of Uganda." PhD diss., Florida State University Tallahassee.

Kagwa, Sir Apolo. 1934. *The Customs of the Baganda.* Translated by Ernest B. Kalibala. New York: Columbia University Press.

———. 1949. *Ekitabo Kye Bika bya Baganda* [A book about the clans of the Baganda]. Kampala: Uganda Bookshop.

———. 1952. *Ekitabo Kye Mpisa Za Baganda* [A book about the customs of the Baganda]. Kampala: Uganda Bookshop.

———. 1971. *Ekitabo kya basekabaka be Buganda, na be Bunyoro, na be Koki, na be Toro, na be Nkole* [The book of the kings of Buganda, Bunyoro, Koki, Toro, and Nkore]. Nairobi: East African Publishing House.

Kaminski, Joseph S. 2012. *Asante Ntahera Trumpets in Ghana: Culture, Tradition, and Sound Barrage.* New York: Routledge.

Kasirye, Joseph S. 1959. *Abateregga ku Nnamulondo ya Buganda* [Heirs to the throne of Buganda], rev. ed. London: Macmillan.

Kasozi, A. B. K. 2013. *The Bitter Bread of Exile: The Financial Problems of Sir Edward Muteesa II during His Final Exile, 1966–1969.* Kampala: Progressive Publishing House.

Katamba, Francis, and Peter Cooke. 1987. "Ssematimba ne Kikwabanga: The Music and Poetry of a Ganda Historical Song." *World of Music* 29 (2): 49–68.

Keller, Janet Dixon, and Takaronga Kuautonga. 2007. *Nokonofo Kitea, We Keep on Living This Way: Myths and Music of Futuna, Vanuatu.* Honolulu: University of Hawai'i Press.

Kirega-Gava, V. P. 2006. *Abaganda n'Olutalo lwa Federo* [The Baganda and the federal debate]. Kampala: Self-published.

Kiingi, K. B. 2007. *Enkuluze ya Oluganda eya e Makerere* [Luganda dictionary of Makerere]. Kampala: Fountain Publishers.

Kiwalabye, S. Dennis. 2008. *Empologoma ya Buganda: The Most Subtle and Powerful Modern Kingdom in Sub-Saharan Africa,* edited by N. Mutumba. Kampala: n.p.

Kiwanuka, M. S. M. Semakula. 1971. *The Kings of Buganda.* Kampala: East African Publishing House.

———. 1972. *A History of Buganda: From the Foundation of the Kingdom to 1900.* New York: African Publishing Corporation.

Kizza, Immaculate N. 2010. *The Oral Tradition of the Baganda of Uganda.* Jefferson, NC: McFarland.

Kodesh, Neil. 2010. *Beyond the Royal Gaze: Clanship and Public Healing in Buganda.* Charlottesville: University of Virginia Press.

Kruger, Jaco. 2007. "Singing Psalms with Owls: A Venda 20th Century Musical History Part Two: Tshikona, Beer Songs and Personal Songs." *African Music* 8 (1): 36–59.

Kubik, Gerhard. 1960. "The Structure of Kiganda Xylophone Music." *African Music* 2 (3): 131–65.

———. 1964. "Xylophone Playing in Southern Uganda." *Journal of the Royal Anthropological Institute of Great Britain and Ireland* 94 (2): 138–59.

———. 1968. "Court Music in Uganda." *Bulletin of the International Committee on Urgent Anthropological and Ethnological Research* 10: 41–51.

———. 1969. "Compositional Techniques in Kiganda Xylophone Music—With an Introduction into Some Kiganda Musical Concepts." *African Music* 4 (3): 22–72.

———. 1998. "Intra-African Streams of Influence." In *The Garland Encyclopedia of World Music, Vol. 1: Africa,* edited by Ruth M. Stone, 293–325. New York: Routledge.

Kulubya, S. W. 1942. "Some Aspects of Baganda Customs." *Uganda Journal* 9 (2): 49–56.

Lévi-Strauss, Claude. 1969. *The Raw and the Cooked.* Translated by John and Doreen Weightman. New York: Harper & Row.

———. 1982. *The Way of the Masks.* Translated by S. Modelski. Seattle: University of Washington Press.

Lush, A. J. 1935. "Kiganda Drums." *Uganda Journal* 3 (1): 7–25.

Makubuya, James Kika. 1995. "Endongo: The Role and Significance of the Baganda Bowl Lyre of Uganda." PhD diss., University of California, Los Angeles.

———. 1999. "The Ndongo Bowl Lyre of the Baganda of Uganda: An Examination of Its Sonic Properties." *African Music* 7 (4): 22–28.

———. 2000. "*Endingidi* (Tube fiddle of Uganda): Its Adaptation and Significance among the Baganda." *Galpin Society Journal* 53: 140–55.

Martin, Denis-Constant. 2013. *Sounding the Cape: Music, Identity and Politics in South Africa.* Somerset West, South Africa: African Minds.

Mawanda, Moses Kazibwe. 1999. *Omuganda ne Kabaka* [The Muganda and the king]. Kampala: Angelina Bookshop.

Merriam, Alan P. 1964. *The Anthropology of Music.* Evanston, IL: Northwestern University Press.

Mushengyezi, Arron. 2007. *Oral Literature for Children: Rethinking Orality, Literacy, Performance, and Documentation Practices.* Amsterdam: Rodopi.

Mutibwa, Phares. 2008. *The Buganda Factor in Uganda Politics.* Kampala: Fountain Publishers.

Muwanga, Jozef S. B. 2005. *On the Kabaka's Road for Uganda: A Contribution to the Positive Mind of Buganda.* Kampala: LDC Publishers.

Nakazibwe, Venny M. 2005. "Bark-cloth of the Baganda People of Southern Uganda: A Record of Continuity and Change from the Late Eighteenth Century to the Early Twenty-first Century." PhD diss., Middlesex University, London.

Nannyonga-Tamusuza, Sylvia A. 2005. *Baakisimba: Gender in the Music and Dance of the Baganda People of Uganda.* New York: Routledge.

Nattiez, Jean-Jacques, and Sylvia A. Nannyonga-Tamusuza. 2005. "Rythme, danse et sexualité: une danse ougandaise d'initiation au mariage" [Rhythm, dance and sex: a Ugandan dance of initiation to marriage]. In *Musiques: Une Encylopédie pour le XXI siècle,* vol. 3, *Musique et culture,* 1108–29. Arles-Paris: Actes Sud-Cité de la Musique.

Nsimbi, M. B. 1956. *Amannya Amaganda n'Ennono Zaago* [Kiganda names and their origins]. Kampala: East African Literature Bureau.

Nsobya, Bro. A. Tarcis. 2000. *Ennono n'Enkulaakulana ya Buganda okuva Ensi nga Eyitibwa Muwawa okutuuka ku Kuyitibwa Buganda ne ku Kwefuga kwa Uganda (400 A.D.–1971)* [The customs and development of Buganda: from when the nation was called Muwawa to when it came to be known as Buganda and into Uganda's independence (400 A.D.–1971)] Kisubi, Uganda: Marianum Press.

Odhiambo, E. S. Atieno, T. I. Ouso, and J. F. M. Williams. 1977. *A History of East Africa.* London: Longman.

Philips, John Edward. 2005. *Writing African History.* Rochester, NY: University of Rochester Press.

Pryor, Tom. 2007. "Mamadou Diabate: The Griot in Your Backyard," *Sing Out!* 51 (2): 41–46.

Radcliffe-Brown, A. R. 1952. *Structure and Function in Primitive Society.* New York: Free Press.

Ray, Benjamin C. 1991. *Myth, Ritual and Kingship in Buganda.* New York: Oxford University Press.

Roscoe, John. 1911. *The Baganda.* London: Macmillan.

Sackeyfio-Lenoch, Naaborko. 2014. *The Politics of Chieftaincy: Authority and Property in Colonial Ghana, 1920–1950.* Rochester, NY: University of Rochester Press.

Sahlins, Marshall. 2011. "What Kinship Is (Part One)." *Journal of the Royal Anthropological Institute* 17 (1): 2–19.

Schieffelin, E. L. 1985. "Performance and the Cultural Construction of Reality." *American Ethnologist* 12: 707–24.

Schneider, David. 1984. *A Critique of the Study of Kinship.* Ann Arbor: University of Michigan Press.

Sempebwa, Ernest K. K. 2004. *Ensozi n'Ebiwonvu n'Emiseetwe: Ebitono ku Bifa ku Mulembe Omuteesa II* [Mountains, valleys, and plains: brief information about the reign of Muteesa II]. Kampala: Wavah Books.

Ssekamwa, J. C. 2001. *Buganda n'Obwakabaka* [Buganda and kingship]. 2nd ed. Kisubi, Uganda: Marianum Press.

———. 2007. *The Buganda Kingdom and Its Monarchy: A Contribution of Nkumba University.* Entebbe, Uganda: Nkumba University.

Ssemakula, Mukasa. "The Territory of Buganda." http://www.buganda.com/masaza.htm; accessed September 5, 2017.

Stephens, Rhiannon. 2013. *A History of African Motherhood: The Case of Uganda, 700–1900.* New York: Cambridge University Press.

Thomson, Alex. 2016. *An Introduction to African Politics.* New York: Routledge.

Ttendo, Bugagga Mutale. 2002. *Ekika ky'Enkima: Ennono n'Emirimu Gyakyo Mu Lubiri* [The Monkey Clan: its customs and duties in the palace]. Kampala: Ttesupa Booklex.

Tumusiime, James. 1992. *Uganda 30 Years, 1962–1992.* Kampala: Fountain Publishers.

Turner, Victor. 1967. *The Forest of Symbols: Aspects of Ndembu Ritual.* Ithaca, NY: Cornell University Press.

———. 1969. *The Ritual Process: Structure and Anti-Structure.* Chicago: Aldine.

Vasquez, Manuel. 2011. *More Than Belief: A Materialist Theory of Religion.* Oxford: Oxford University Press.

Wagner, Roy. 1977. "Analogic Kinship: A Daribi Example." *American Ethnologist* 4 (4): 623–42.

Ward, Kevin. 1991. "A History of Christianity in Uganda." In *From Mission to Church: A Handbook of Christianity in East Africa,* edited by Zablon Nthamburi. Nairobi: Uzima Press.

———. 1998. "The Church of Uganda and the Exile of Kabaka Muteesa II, 1953–55." *Journal of Religion in Africa* 28 (4): 411–49.

Wachsmann, Klaus P. 1953. "The Sound Instruments." In *Tribal Crafts of Uganda,* edited by Margaret Trowell and Klaus P. Wachsmann, 311–415. London: Oxford University Press.

———. 1971. "Musical Instruments in the Kiganda Tradition and Their Place in the East African Scene." In *Essays on Music and History in Africa,* edited by Klaus Wachsmann, 93–134. Evanston, IL: Northwestern University Press.

Wavamunno, Gordon 2004. *Nnabulagala/Kasubi, Naggalabi/Buddo and Kabaale/ Kkungu: The Traditional Places in Buganda.* Kampala: Wavah Books.

———. 2007. *Ssekabaka Muteesa II, President wa Uganda eyasooka era omulwanirizi w'emirembe kayingo* [Ssekabaka Muteesa II, the first president of Uganda as well as an outstanding defender of peace]. Kampala: Wavah Books.

Wilcken, Lois. 1992. *The Drums of Vodou.* New York: White Cliffs Media.

Wrigley, Christopher. 1996. *Kingship and State: The Buganda Dynasty.* Cambridge: Cambridge University Press.

Index

Page numbers in italics indicate illustrations or musical examples. Please refer to the glossary (pp. 111–21) for definitions of non-English terms.